THE CORE
STRONG FOUNDATIONS OF FAITH

OLD COVENANT AND ANCIENT ISRAEL

REV. CHARLIE HOLT

Old Covenant and Ancient Israel
The Core: Strong Foundations of Faith

© 2022 by The Rev. Charlie Holt
Published in Jacksonville, Florida by Bible Study Media, Inc.

All rights reserved. No part of this publication may be reproduced, distributed, or transmitted in any form or by any means, including photocopying, recording, or other electronic or mechanical methods, without the prior written permission of the publisher, except in the case of brief quotations embodied in critical reviews and certain other noncommercial uses permitted by copyright law.

Unless otherwise indicated, Scripture quotations are from the ESV® Bible (The Holy Bible, English Standard Version®), copyright © 2001 by Cross-way, a publishing ministry of Good News Publishers. Used by permission. All rights reserved.

ISBN Number: 978-1-942243-62-5
Library of Congress Control Number: 2022916185

TABLE OF CONTENTS

Introduction to the Core	5
Introduction to the Old Covenant and Ancient Israel	9
Chapter 1 Exodus: The Founding of Israel	11
Chapter 2 Name: The God of Abraham, Isaac and Jacob	31
Chapter 3 Torah: The Law of Moses	47
Chapter 4 Temple: The Kingdom of Priests	65
Chapter 5 Promised Land: The Conquest	85
Chapter 6 King: God's Anointed One	103
Chapter 7 Prophet: The Word of the Lord	127
Chapter 8 Restoration: Exile and Return	145
Chapter 9 Wisdom of Israel: The Fear of the Lord	163

A Wandering Aramean

Fig. 1. Molnar, Jozsef. *Abraham's Jouney from Ur to Canaan*. 1850. Oil on canvas. Hungarian National Gallery, Budapest.

> "A wandering Aramean was my father.
>
> And he went down into Egypt and sojourned there, few in number, and there he became a nation, great, mighty and populous.
>
> And the Egyptians treated us harshly and humiliated us and laid on us hard labor.
>
> Then we cried to the LORD, the God of our fathers, and the LORD heard our voice and saw our affliction, our toil and our oppression.
>
> And the LORD brought us out of Egypt with a mighty hand and an outstretched arm, with great deeds of terror, with signs and wonders.
>
> And he brought us into this place and gave us this land, the land flowing with milk and honey.
>
> And behold, now I bring you the first of the fruit of the ground, which you, O LORD, have given me."
>
> *Deuteronomy 26:5-10*

INTRODUCTION TO THE CORE
Strong Foundations of Faith

The Core is a course of study designed to help the maturing Christian develop a strong foundation for lifelong learning. The mature disciple of Jesus Christ will be able to express the Christian worldview with truth and love as they witness to their faith in the world.

The Christian worldview is all-encompassing. It affirms our identity in Christ, purpose in life, character, and ethics. It develops over a lifetime. Christians are called to develop a broad, inclusive—and even sophisticated—view of life. This view has at its core a relationship with God and other people. It reflects the phenomenon of human existence as well as a person's philosophical, "moral" and religious positions based on deep reflection upon, and relationship with, God's word as revealed in the Bible.

The Christian worldview encourages deep thought about fundamental questions such as the origins of the universe, development of life, the nature of good and evil, and the ultimate destiny of all things. These first-order concepts then lead to questions, understandings and applications for the nature of individual development, family dynamics, the relationship between church and state, social challenges, and the world of politics and economics.

"The Christian worldview encourages deep thought about fundamental questions such as the origins of the universe, development of life, the nature of good and evil, and the ultimate destiny of all things."

In order to build a solid foundation for the Christian worldview, we will explore the breadth of Christian knowledge, understanding, and wisdom through a study of six key areas of Christian theology and practice.

The six classes are:

1. Old Covenant and Ancient Israel
2. New Covenant and the Early Christian Church
3. Christian History and Theology
4. Christian Formation and Spiritual Practice
5. Contemporary Christian Ethics and Apologetics
6. Christian Vocation and Servant-Leadership

All the classes in *The Core* will combine to create a comprehensive understanding of the basics of Christianity. For example, to understand the new covenant and early church, one must have prior knowledge and understanding of the old covenant and ancient Israel. How does the exodus from Egypt help explain the cross and resurrection of Jesus? Why does Jesus redefine the Jewish passover meal to apply to his sacrificed body and blood? How does the sacrificial system of Solomon's temple relate to the new living temple in Paul's letter to the Ephesians? We will consider the importance of these questions in the modern day, and we will answer them.

From a broad grasp of the teaching of the entire Bible, we can build a theological understanding and rule of life for spiritual formation and practice. The sacramental life established by Jesus and the Apostles is manifest in the contemporary community of the Church. It leads to individual as well as communal maturity.

Finally, through *The Core*, the maturing Christian will learn how to engage in the world as a wise advocate for the Christian faith and as a compelling servant-leader. How does a mature Christian interact with the larger marketplace of ideas and religious paradigms? The call and vocation of the Christian is to consider every thought as we contend for the Gospel in a world that does not understand its value and at times is even hostile to its central message.

By working through each of *The Core's* six courses, the Christian student will gain a foundation for future study. We will offer interpretive keys to Biblical passages that will allow for far greater exploration in the future. Along the way, we will share other tools that will always be of great use to the Christian. And if this course is done in community, the participants will make friends who can share their faith journey and live shoulder to shoulder with them in the faith. Ultimately, the aim of the core curriculum is to help bring all people closer to Jesus in ways that will change their world for good.

The Core Series: The Beginning

It is natural for all human beings to try to come to a better understanding of the world around them. However, unlike God, we know very little about it; and so, we find that we need to base many of our observations upon assumptions about what those observations mean. These assumptions are *core*, because they shape the entire way we view the world.

It should be little surprise, then, that when we attempt to teach another person about a topic, there will be core assumptions that shape the content and manner of that teaching. This should be remembered by those who wish to study Christianity: many Christian learners never consider or examine the assumptions made by those who teach them. As a result, they can be led astray if their teacher has faulty beliefs about the faith.

For example, if a Biblical scholar were an atheist, then their scholarship would inevitably reflect their belief that there is no God. One such popular scholar is Dr. Bart Ehrman, James A. Gray Distinguished Professor of Religious Studies at the University of North Carolina at Chapel Hill, who offers one of his core assumptions (and its logical implication):

"I came to a point where I simply didn't believe there was a God who was active in the world, and that necessarily had implications, because there can't be a miraculous resurrection of Jesus if there's nobody who is performing miracles." [1]

Because of this assumption, Ehrman would reject the claim that an act of God could be considered, or even classified, as an historical event. His worldview is implicitly and explicitly reflected in his writings:

"You've moved from history to faith,' he objects. 'You can show historically that people claimed they saw Jesus alive afterwards, you can draw the conclusion that they probably believed it. But if you yourself agree that Jesus was raised from the dead, you are saying that was an act of God in history. What you are doing is no longer history – it's faith." [2]

Therefore, a scholar such as Ehrman will teach the miracle stories of the resurrection as mere human myth with no historic basis—a conclusion which by his own admission is governed by his starting assumption. If there is no God, then there is no way that a person could miraculously come back to life after three days. There must be some other explanation for the story.

For many secular historians, faith in the rules and conventions of modern history and science preclude any possibility of Jesus' divinity and miracles such as his resurrection. When asked why an historian would not even consider the real possibility that the resurrection actually happened, Dr. Dale Martin, Woolsey Professor Emeritus of Religious Studies, Yale University, responds:

"What can the modern historian say about the historical Jesus and not lose tenure. You can't say Jesus is divine if you are a modern historian. We can't say for example that the resurrection of Jesus is a historical fact. Nobody who accepts modern science can accept that." [3]

Might it be true, however, that the core assumptions of modern science and modern history are flawed, or even simply wrong? Are their rules and presuppositions beyond question?

The scholarly expositions of the Bible by atheist scholars like Bart Ehrman and Dale Martin are shaped around explanations, propositions and conclusions that merely expand the key core assumption—that there is no God. Unreflective students of scholars like these may unknowingly accept their unspoken and unsupported assumptions. The house built on sand may be quite appealing. But a sharp, critically-minded person will not enter that house without asking some questions first!

Of course, the same argument could sometimes be applied to believing scholars. One cannot escape the fact that thought is always shaped by core assumptions. That's just how it is. And sometimes, people's assumptions change radically over time. This movement from one set of core assumptions to another is the act of *conversion*. Such conversions are often shaped by factors beyond the scope of reasonable argument and thought. As Blase Pascal famously wrote in his *Pensées*,[4] "The heart has its reasons, which reason does not know. We feel it in a thousand things. It is the heart which experiences God, and not the reason. This, then, is faith: God felt by the heart, not by the reason."[4] Bart Ehrman's conversion from believing in God to rejecting God required no less faith than C.S. Lewis' conversion, after many years of rejecting God, he surrendered to belief.

"You must picture me alone in that room at Magdalen, night after night, feeling, whenever my mind lifted even for a second from my work, the steady, unrelenting approach of Him whom I so earnestly desired not to meet. That which I greatly feared had at last come upon me. In the Trinity Term of 1929 I gave in, and admitted that God was God, and knelt and prayed: perhaps, that night, the most dejected and reluctant convert in all England." [5]

Jesus' resurrection, like it or not, is a matter of historic fact. It either happened or it didn't. Our core assumptions can do nothing to change that. Yet, the core beliefs residing deep in the human heart will influence and determine our understanding and view of the world and our significance within it. So let's go to *The Core*.

---

[1] Brierley, Justin, "The Sceptic: Why I Can't Believe The Resurrection." Premier Christianity, May 1, 2014, https://www.premierchristianity.com/Past-Issues/2014/May-2014/The-Sceptic-Why-I-can-t-believe-the-resurrection

[2] Ibid.

[3] Hinge Podcast, Interview with Dale Martin, "#1 It was my job to have answers", December 14, 2017.

[4] Blasé Pascal, Pensées, (E. P. Dutton & Co., Inc.., 1958), Of the Means of Belief, 277-278.

[5] Surprised By Joy, (Harper Collins, 1955), chapter 14, page 266.

INTRODUCTION TO THE OLD COVENANT AND ANCIENT ISRAEL

The key for our study of Old and New Testament books is to be aware of and honest about our assumptions. Wisdom can discern core assumptions in others, and when we are studying the writings of archeologists, scholars, preachers, and teachers we must always be attuned to the fact that their works are always informed by their beliefs whether they explicitly state them or not. To that end, we begin by offering several starting assumptions as core for believing Christians as they approach the study of the Bible.

The Authority of the Bible

As Christians, we read the Bible with believing eyes and trusting hearts. Our understanding is that God indeed exists, and that he has spoken and is speaking to us through the written text of the Bible. The Bible is authoritative on matters of Christian belief and morality and deeply practical and useful for mature and abundant faith and life.

The Apostle Paul writes in his second letter to Timothy,

"All Scripture is breathed out by God and profitable for teaching, for reproof, for correction, and for training in righteousness, that the man of God may be complete, equipped for every good work." (2 Timothy 3:16)

Not every student and scholar of the Bible takes this view. Many people see the Bible as an interesting and even important work of literature. But they accept it neither as a moral authority nor as the revealed word of God. The field of Christian apologetics addresses the challenges these people raise, using reasonable arguments to defend the Christian worldview. We will study apologetics in depth in the fifth course. For now, let us simply approach the text of the Bible with Christian humility.

The Literary Unity of the Bible and its Individual Books

The Bible has two main sections: the Old and New Covenants (or Testaments). Together, these Covenants contain 66 unique books, which have many authors who wrote at various times. These books have several functions expressed in many different genres such as narrative, poetry, law, prophecy, and letters. Each one of those books should be considered a complete literary work unto itself. However, the individual books all relate to one another and come together in one overarching narrative.

The Bible, even with its many distinct parts, is a unified literary whole. Prophecies in earlier books are fulfilled in later ones. Biblical writers constantly quote, paraphrase, and comment on each other's passages. Throughout, the many literary genres interact beautifully and naturally with a Spirit-inspired synergy. The Bible has a beginning, a middle, and an end. It has major and minor characters, heroes and villains, love and conflict, and a central plot, which is God's willingness to bring the ultimate salvation of humanity in and through his son Jesus Christ.

A mature Christian can discern the rich diversity of the books and the literary unity of the Bible as a key principle of its faithful interpretation. Nothing is there by chance: it is all inspired by God himself, and it all fits together for our learning and growth in the faith.

The Context of the Bible

Finally, as Christians, we believe that we must interpret the Bible in its original context prior to application to the contemporary world.

The original writers of the Bible were concerned with addressing the specific needs, hopes and concerns of their audience, "time," and culture. That does not at all mean that the scriptures do not apply to us—they most certainly do! However, it does mean that if we are to faithfully understand and apply it today, we must start by learning how it was understood and applied back then.

Essential to an educated understanding of Scripture is a consideration of various contexts, especially the historical, geographic, and cultural contexts of each book.

The *historical context* analyzes political movements such as the rise and fall of key historic figures and events of the times such as kings, tribal rulers, and significant battles. Our knowledge of Biblical history often comes from sources such as original ancient historians and the archeological record.

The *geographic context* includes a knowledge of ancient settings such as Mesopotamia, Canaan, Egypt, Israel, Assyria, Babylon, Asia Minor, Greece, and Rome. A faithful interpretation of the Bible will develop proper awareness of the places described, using historic maps and other tools that show crucial elements of the story, such as relationships between bodies of water, trade routes, geo-political boundaries, topography, and locations of key cities.

The *cultural context* encourages consideration of the societies in which the people of the Bible lived. For example, most of the cultures in the Old Covenant were patriarchal in family structure. By and large, they owned slaves. With the exception of Israel, they were polytheistic, worshipping a pantheon of gods. Kings, emperors and tribal warlords dominated the political scene. War and violence, rather intermittent and noteworthy in much of the world today, were simply a constant presence in life back then.

We recognize that the Bible speaks through the historical, geographic, and cultural idiosyncrasies of its original context, and therefore will resonate with cultural markers. For example, it would make little sense to expect the creation narrative to speak in the voice of a 21st century physics textbook, or for the original language of the text to reflect the politically correct norms of our day regarding gender pronouns. That is simply not the context in which it was written—which does not make its message any less true today. Our challenge is to make appropriate adjustments to our interpretations of certain historical, cultural, and theological aspects of the Bible in order to apply it to our context, all while remaining faithful to God in the interpretive process!

The Dance of Hermeneutics and Exegesis

Hermeneutics is a discipline of study that focuses on principles of interpretation of literary and particularly Biblical texts. It is closely related to the discipline of exegesis, which is the science of correctly determining what a text says. Hermeneutics would more broadly consider what a text means and how it applies today. One way to simply put it, exegesis answers the question, "what does the text say?". Hermeneutics answers the broader question, "what does the text mean?"

These two disciplines of Biblical study interrelate, and synergistically inform one another. All exegesis involves hermeneutical decisions, and all hermeneutics requires solid clear exegesis. An educated reader of Scripture is attuned to these two disciplines and how they always dance together.

CHAPTER 1
Exodus: The Founding of Israel

OBJECTIVE: The Old Testament is an essential component in the framework of a Christian worldview. We will begin by examining how it is organized, how it works, and what it offers to Christian faith and life.

Multiple Perspectives

Imagine for a moment that you are watching a football game. If you were watching the game in person, you may have a limited perspective from the bleachers. Such a perspective is, of course, a real one; however, if you were watching it on television, you would have access to multiple perspectives, which would provide you with a more complete understanding of the game. On TV, there are several camera angles and fields of vision: one camera might have a high-resolution close-up shot of the quarterback throwing the ball; another could capture the entire field of play, showing all the players but with far less detail. With replay, crucial moments of the game can be highlighted. Seasoned experts provide interpretation of the plays and commentary on the players. There is the possibility of an interview with a coach or player after the game. These different perspectives alternately reveal, limit, focus and highlight the game in order to present a full picture.

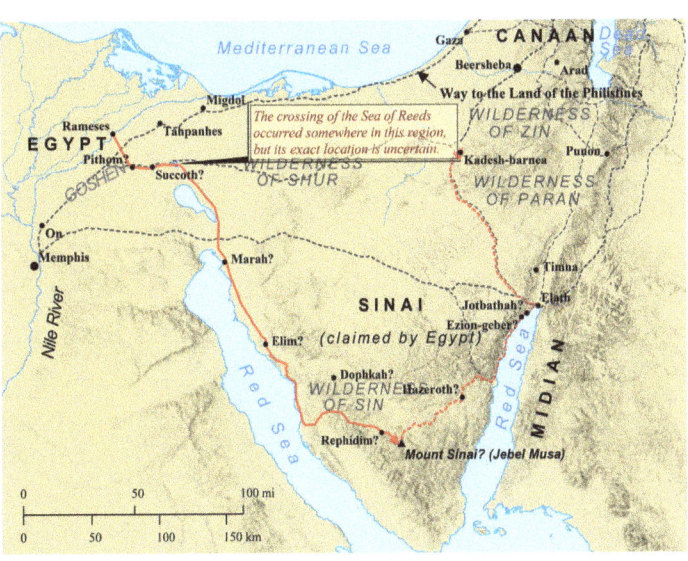

Map 1. *Created with BibleMapper.com 5.0.* Used with permission.

In the same way, we can look at the Bible through multiple lenses and perspectives. One of these perspectives is the *literary perspective*. This perspective involves studying each book of the Bible as a literary unit, complete with its own writer, genre, and audience. Elements like character development, plot, and literary structure are of particular interest, as would be the context of the author and the original audience.

Another approach may be to look from a *thematic perspective*. A person studying the Bible thematically might contemplate how a theological theme such as the sinful nature of humanity or the love of God develops over the course of the Bible. One could also follow the story of a particular Biblical figure. For example, a thematic examination of the way that Abraham is portrayed and referenced throughout Scripture could be very fruitful.

A student might also make use of a *canonical perspective*. This perspective asks questions about how the books of the Bible relate to one another. How, say, does the Creation in Genesis influence the writing of the Gospel of John? How do the various books of the Bible all work together as a literary whole? Why are they even in the Bible in the first place, and is there a logic behind the organization of the books?

The most important of these lenses, however, is the *redemptive historical perspective*. This is akin to the wide-angle view of all of the football field; it contains all of the figures in the Bible and identifies the whole of Scripture as the story of how God redeems humanity from sin.

This story of redemption begins with the account of how we came to be separated from God. Our fall from paradise and fellowship with God into rebellion, sin, evil and death is told in the first three chapters of Genesis. The pages of Scripture then show, in great detail, the consequences of the fall, and how God saves humanity from that fall over the course of human history.

In our first chapter, we will adopt the redemptive historical perspective. Although Genesis is the first book of the Old Testament, the second book—Exodus—narrates how God gave his people the old covenant. As an act of God in redemptive history, the exodus stands apart as the defining moment for ancient Israel. The nation of Israel would not exist today were it not for the Exodus from Egypt. The Exodus is the interpretive key that can unlock understanding of the Old Testament, and it serves as the primary metaphor for understanding the story of the entire Bible.

BEGIN AT THE END: Tithe First Fruits

Deuteronomy 26:1-4 instructs the Jewish people on how to make the proper offering after the first harvest. The very best yields of their crops, the top 10 percent, was to be taken to the temple and given to the priest with these words:

"I declare today to the Lord your God that I have come into the land that the LORD swore to our fathers to give us." By these words, the people

would remember their humble beginnings, and celebrate that they have a home, by the gracious and powerful hand of God. Their tithe of the first fruit of the harvest is Israel's response to God's redemption, deliverance and blessing. Every time the tithe was placed at the altar, the worshiper would recite this creed:

"A wandering Aramean was my father. And he went down into Egypt and sojourned there, few in number, and there he became a nation, great, mighty and populous. And the Egyptians treated us harshly and humiliated us and laid on us hard labor. Then we cried to the LORD, the God of our fathers, and the LORD heard our voice and saw our affliction, our toil and our oppression. And the LORD brought us out of Egypt with a mighty hand and an outstretched arm, with great deeds of terror, with signs and wonders. And he brought us into this place and gave us this land, the land flowing with milk and honey. And behold, now I bring you the first of the fruit of the ground, which you, O LORD, have given me." (Deuteronomy 26:5-10)

Creedal Statement

Can you imagine the immense power behind that statement? Every time a tithe was offered, the story of the Exodus was retold in the people's minds: "I am so grateful to God because I know where I came from. I know that I came from humble beginnings, that the Lord did something awesome for me. He brought me out of slavery, out of bondage, out of cruelty and tyranny. He gave me an amazing, abundant land here. My best 10 percent, I give back to the Lord for what he has done for me."

A Wandering Aramean

Fig. 1. Molnar, Jozsef. ***Abraham's Jouney from Ur to Canaan***. 1850. Oil on canvas. Hungarian National Gallery, Budapest.

Every Israelite knew that they would be no one, have nothing, and live nowhere, if it were not for the Exodus. In positive terms, the Exodus defines their identity and gives them a value and a place. The Exodus made Israel the beloved people of God, the heirs to a glorious inheritance. One could argue that the Exodus is for the Old Testament what the cross and resurrection is for the New Testament. It is the redemptive, historical moment for the Israelites that defines everything for them. It is what makes Israel special.

A Wandering Aramean

In the beginning of Exodus, the Israelites are no more than the family of Jacob, the descendants of Abraham. The verse, *"A wandering Aramean was my father"* (Deuteronomy 26:5) is a reference to Abraham.

CHAPTER 1   Exodus: The Founding of Israel   15

From Abraham, the line passes down to his son Isaac and his grandson Jacob, who had 12 sons. The patriarchs of Israel were nomadic wanderers and herdsmen who lived in tents, not unlike modern-day Bedouins. Jacob, his sons and their households numbered 70 people when they entered Egypt, leaving their home in Aram, in northern Syria. One of Jacob's sons was already there: Joseph had been sold into slavery by his own jealous brothers several years before. After God blesses Joseph and protects him through several misadventures, he used the ability God had given him to interpret dreams. Through this gift, he was elevated to become second-in-command of the pharaoh's Egyptian kingdom. He had the Egyptians store massive amounts of food, because of a terrible famine that had been predicted through the Pharaoh's dreams. Joseph's family, struggling for food, eventually reunited with him, after traveling through the land of Canaan and into the northern regions of Egypt, to a land called Goshen.

Fig. 2.

Over a period of about 430 years, Joseph dies, the patriarchs die and the pharaoh who knew Joseph also dies. During these years, Abraham's descendants became very numerous:

"But the people of Israel were fruitful and increased greatly; They multiplied and grew exceedingly strong, so that the land was filled with them." (Exodus 1:7)

The new pharaoh doesn't know anything about Joseph or what he did for Egypt and feels threatened by the sizable and growing population of Hebrews.

Hebrew Midwives

The pharaoh decides that the Israelites are so numerous that they pose a security threat to Egypt. He decrees to the Hebrew midwives, *"When you serve as midwife to the Hebrew women and see them on the birthstool, if it is a son, you shall kill him, but if it is a daughter, she shall live."* (Exodus 1:16) Male children were a potential warrior population; female children were allowed to live because they could be married to Egyptians and more easily assimilated into Egyptian society.

The Hebrew midwives, however, feared God more than the pharaoh, and let the boys live. When the king of Egypt asks the midwives why they have let the Hebrew children live, the midwives answer, *"Because the Hebrew women are not like the Egyptian women, for they are vigorous and give birth before the midwife comes to them."* (Exodus 1:19) And so again, the people multiplied and became very numerous.

In response, the pharaoh decreed that all of the Hebrew male babies were to be thrown into the Nile River—which leads to the story of Moses. As a baby, Moses was placed by his family in a small raft into the Nile, where one of the princesses of Egypt discovers him and raises him as a prince.

Fig. 3. *The Birth of Moses, the Crusader Bible.* 1240s. Illuminated manuscript. Morgan Library & Museum, New York.

Cruel Bondage

The tithing creed continues, *"And the Egyptians treated us harshly, and humiliated us, and laid on us hard labor."* (Deuteronomy 26:6)

Fig. 4. *Making bricks in ancient Egypt: The tomb of Vizier Rekhmire.* ca. 1450 BCE. Facsimile painting by Nina de Garis Davies. Courtesy of the Metropolitan Museum of Art, Rogers Fund.

The Exodus story tells us that the Hebrews were forced to make the bricks for the pharaoh's storage cities.

They cried out to the Lord to rescue them from slavery, and he heard

CHAPTER 1 Exodus: The Founding of Israel 17

Fig. 5. Bourdon, Sebastien. *Moses and the Burning Bush*. 1642-1645. Oil on canvas. Hermitage Museum, St. Petersburg/Bridgeman Images.

them. God remembered his covenant with Abraham, Isaac and Jacob, and raised Moses to deliver his people.

God sent Moses into the desert of Midian, where he came to a mountain called Sinai (or Meron or Mount Moriah). There Moses saw a bush on fire, though it was not consumed by the fire. The presence of the angel of the Lord was in the bush and Moses spoke to the Lord directly. The Lord told him that he was standing on holy ground, saying, *"I have surely seen the affliction of my people who are in Egypt and I have heard their cry because of their taskmasters. I know their sufferings and I've come down to deliver them out of the hand of the Egyptians and to bring them up out of that land to a good and broad land, a land flowing with milk and honey…"* (Exodus 3:7-8)

TEN PLAGUES: Victory over Spiritual and Worldly Oppressors

After his encounter with God, Moses returns to challenge the pharaoh. The creed describes God's judgment: *"The LORD brought us out of Egypt with a mighty hand and an outstretched arm, with great deeds of terror and signs of wonders."* (Deuteronomy 26:8)

A repeating cycle emerges from the encounters between Moses and the pharaoh: Moses asks the pharaoh, *"Let my people go."* With a heart hardened to the Lord, the pharaoh refuses. God then sends his judgment down on Egypt with a plague. God's first judgment was turning the water of the Nile River into blood; then he sends frogs; then gnats; and so on for seven more plagues. Interestingly, each of these plagues demonstrates God's authority and ability to destroy any and all of Egypt's gods at will.

As the plagues become more and more severe, the pharaoh becomes more willing to let the Israelites go, and comes very close to doing so at one point. However, God hardened the pharaoh's heart, and did not allow him to repent. Thus, God's mighty hand was fully displayed, letting the people of the world know that all of the Egyptian gods were utterly powerless before the one true God, Yahweh.

PASSOVER: Redemption

The tenth and most severe judgment was the Passover, the death of

THE TEN PLAGUES OF EGYPT
The Judgement of Yahweh on Egypt's Gods

The pantheon of Egyptian gods numbered more than 2,000. Each of the plagues attacked multiple gods as well as the economic, agricultural and food stock wellbeing of the country. Each plague seems to be progressively worse than the previous ones. Only the first three affected the people of Egypt and the people of Goshen (the Israelites). After the second plague, Pharaoh's magicians are unable to duplicate the actions of Moses. After the Boils, they are never seen again.

PLAGUES	GODS OF EGYPT	JUDGEMENT
1 **Water Turned to Blood** Exodus 7:14-25	**Khnum:** Guardian of the River Nile's source **Hapi:** Spirit of the Nile & it's dynamic essence **Osiris:** God of the underworld; Nile was his bloodstream	The Nile was not only a source of water and food but also a major transportation route for agriculture and trade. The putrid smell and toxic nature of this plague made most of these things impossible. Without the Nile, Egypt could not survive.
2 **Frogs** Exodus 8:1-15	**Heqet:** Frog goddess of Nile. Wife of Khnum. Symbol of resurrection and fertility.	Frogs were sacred. Yahweh turned something significant into something loathsome.
3 **Lice** Exodus 8:16-19	**Geb:** The earth god of Egypt. Worshiped for bounty of the soil	The soil became the pestilence. The priesthood could not tolerate being soiled by the gnats (lice); the temple was violated (made unclean) and they could not enter.
4 **Flies** Exodus 8:20-32	**Uatchit:** The fly god of Egypt. Gave protection against disease or misfortune	Under this plague, all of Egypt experienced the wrath of Yahweh.
5 **Disease of Livestock & Animals** Exodus 9:1-7	**Ptah:** Creator of the moon, sun and earth **Hathor:** Goddess of love **Mnevis:** A sacred bull **Amun (Ra):** God of the sun and air **Khnum:** The ram god **Bast:** The cat goddess of love	Many gods were worshiped through animals. In this plague, all manner of livestock is killed, including cows, bulls, horses, camels and donkeys. These animals were key to the economy and provided transport and trade. Also, a large herd was a sign of wealth. Yahweh wiped them out.
6 **Boils** Exodus 9:8-12	**Sekhmet:** Goddess of epidemics **Serapis:** God of healing **Imhotep:** God of medicine and guardian of the healing sciences	None of the Egyptian gods could stop this plague and it further demonstrated their impotence. The Pharaoh's priests were denied access to their temples for purity reasons. The magicians could not see the Pharaoh due to their affliction of boils.
7 **Hail** Exodus 9:13-35	**Nut:** Sky goddess **Isis & Seth:** Agricultural deities **Shu:** God of the atmosphere	It's likely that only flax and barley were destroyed. However, any farm animal or person outside during the storm died. As well, monuments built to these gods were likely defiled. Again, it speaks to the power of Yahweh and the impotence of the Egyptian gods.
8 **Locusts** Exodus 10:1-20	**Serapia:** Protector from locusts **Nepri:** Goddess of grain **Ermutet:** Goddess of childbirth and crops **Thermuthis:** Goddess of fertility and the harvest **Seth:** God of crops	Food was essential to survival. So far, Yahweh has polluted the Nile and destroyed marine life, wiped out the livestock, and now he destroys the ability to make bread and beer - both staples in the Egyptian diet.
9 **Darkness** Exodus 10:21-29	**Amun Ra:** Chief deity of Egypt **Atun:** A sun diety **Thoth:** God of writing and wisdom, truth and integrity, one of the most important deities in the Egyptian pantheon **Horus:** God of light **Shu:** God of the air and sunlight	Darkness is a direct attack against Pharaoh, the divine representation on earth of Ra the sun god. For three days he could do nothing. Yet, the land of Goshen had light.
10 **Death of Firstborn** Exodus 12:29-36	All the gods of Egypt but especially: **Isis:** Goddess of fertility **Meskhenet:** Goddess of childbirth **Hathor:** A deity that attended the birth of children **Min:** God of procreation **Selket:** Guardian of life **Renenutet:** Goddess and guardian of Pharaoh	This final plague was an attack on all the Egyptian gods. It showed the total inability of them to protect their subjects. Perhaps the worst plague, this one removed the first heir to a father's inheritance and harmed a family legally and emotionally. Finally, it undermined Pharaoh's claim of immorality, since his firstborn would also have been immortal.

Sources
https://www.ancient.eu/article/885/egyptian-gods---the-complete-list/
https://www.knowingthebible.net/yahweh-versus-the-gods-of-egypt

the firstborn. Moses prophesied that the angel of death would pass over Egypt. To protect the Hebrews, he instructed each family to take a lamb without spot or blemish, sacrifice it, and put some of the lamb's blood on the doorpost of their home. In houses without the blood, the firstborn—livestock and children—were killed. But when the angel of death saw the blood on the lintels of the Hebrews' houses, he spared their homes.

"So Moses said, 'Thus says the LORD, 'About midnight I'll go out in the midst of Egypt, and every firstborn in the land of Egypt shall die,

from the firstborn of Pharaoh who sits on his throne, even to the firstborn of the slave girl who is behind the handmill, and all the firstborn of the cattle.

There shall be a great cry throughout all the land of Egypt, such as there has never been, or ever will be again.

But not a dog shall growl against any of the people of Israel, either man or beast, that you may know that the LORD makes a distinction between Egypt and Israel.

And all of these your servants shall come down to me and bow down to me, saying,

Fig. 6. *Passover.* Woodcut. T*he Angel of Death and the First Passover*. (Illustration from the *1897 Bible Pictures and What They Teach Us* by Charles Foster)

'Get out you, and all the people who follow you.' And after that I will go out, and he went out from Pharaoh in hot anger.

Then the LORD said to Moses, 'Pharaoh will not listen to you, that my wonders may be multiplied in the land of Egypt.'

Moses and Aaron did all these wonders before Pharaoh, and the Lord hardened Pharaoh's heart, and he did not let the people of Israel go out of his land." (Exodus 11:4-10)

The angel of death did indeed pass through: *"At midnight, the LORD struck down all the firstborn in the land of Egypt, from the firstborn of*

Pharaoh who sat on his throne, to the firstborn of the captive who was in the dungeon, and the firstborn of the livestock. And Pharaoh rose up in the night he and all of his servants and all the Egyptians. And there was a great cry in Egypt, for there was not a house where someone was not dead. Then he summoned Moses and Aaron by night and said, 'Up, go out from among my people, both you and the people of Israel, and go and serve the LORD, as you have said. Take your flocks and your herds as you have said and be gone and bless me also."
(Exodus 12:29-32)

God promised his people that the Egyptians would not only tell them to leave, they would give them all their gold and silver, and practically beg them to leave. And so the Israelites left slavery with the treasures of Egypt in their possession!

Tohu Va Bohu

One of the key theological elements of the Old Testament is God's formation of a new people, in a new land. He takes them from the chaos in Genesis 1:2. This chaos is known in Hebrew as *tohu va bohu*.

"The earth was without form and void...." (Genesis 1:2) The Earth was a *tohu va bohu*, a formless void. And out of that darkness, God said, *"Let there be light and there was light."* (Genesis. 1:3) And he made an entire creation, ending with rest on the Sabbath, the seventh day. This *creatio ex nihilo* is a prologue for God's work in the Exodus. The wilderness into which the people of Israel escape from Egypt is also called *"a desert land ... in the howling waste of the wilderness;"* (Deuteronomy 32:10). It was a kind of formless void. In contrast, the promised land is referred to throughout the Old Testament and the New Testament as the land of Sabbath rest (See Psalm 95:11 and Hebrews 4:4-11).

Thus, the journey from Egypt into the promised land is a journey of new creation. God took a people who had been completely subjugated by cruel tyranny and bondage and liberated them in order to form a great and mighty nation.

However, before the Israelites can arrive in the promised land, they must undergo a process of purification, which involves 40 years of wandering in the wilderness that will help them to forget the ways of Egypt.

RED SEA CROSSING: Deliverance

As the Lord leads the Israelites to the edge of the Red Sea, the pharaoh changes his mind about letting them go. He pursues them with his army and chariots, surrounding them. The Lord challenges Moses to put his staff into the water. And the sea parts and the Israelites go across on dry ground. Then the water closes on the pursuing army and drowns the pharaoh and his chariot soldiers. In the end, not only are the Egyptians plundered, they also lost their firstborn children and their military. The Exodus is devastating for Egypt.

Fig. 7. *Red Sea crossing*. 1481. Roselli, Cosimo. Sistine Chapel.

There are three phases to the wilderness wanderings. The first two took place early on when God guided the path of the Israelites by a pillar of cloud by day and fire by night. Even though they've seen all the mighty work that God has done—the plagues and the parting of the sea—they are still beholden to a slave mentality, which impedes them from fully trusting God. For centuries, they had been taught to trust the Egyptian gods and the Egyptians as their providers.

The first major scene is when the Israelites experience hunger and thirst, they begin to grumble and complain against Moses. *"Would that we had died by the hand of the LORD in the land of Egypt when we sat by the meat pots and ate bread to the full, for you brought us out into this wilderness to kill the whole assembly with hunger."* (Exodus 16:3) And so Moses cries to the Lord for food. And the Lord miraculously provides manna (a kind of bread) in the wilderness.

In Deuteronomy, the reason that God gave his people manna in the wilderness is revealed: by it, the Israelites would learn that their survival is not dependent upon physical bread and water. People, then as now, are often tempted to trust in the bread of dependency provided by the pharaohs of the world. They forget, however, that the cost of that bread is their freedom.

"And he humbled you and let you hunger and fed you with manna, which you did not know, nor did your fathers know, that he might make you know that man does not live by bread alone, but man lives by every word that comes from the mouth of the LORD." (Deuteronomy 8:3)

For us to have life, and have life abundantly, we must trust in the promise of God's word in our lives. The apostle Peter writes that it is through *"his precious and very great promises, so that through them you may become partakers of the divine nature, having escaped from the corruption that is in the world because of sinful desire."* (2 Peter 1:4) The lesson that we should learn from the Israelites' time in the *tohu va bohu* is to obey the word of God and to trust his providence for deliverance and restoration.

Mount Sinai—Giving of the Law

The second major scene in the wilderness is God's giving of the law at Mount Sinai, when Moses receives the Ten Commandments. Along with these commandments, God also gives him instructions to build an elaborate tabernacle, which would have an ark of the covenant to hold the Ten Commandments. It was designed as the literal dwelling-place of the Lord, where people could go to meet and worship him.

While Moses receives God's word on the mountain, the Israelites are distracted. Impatient with the wait for their leader, they decide to pool all of their gold, melt it, and create a statue of a golden calf, which they then began to worship as the god who delivered them out of Egypt!

Why would the Israelites make a golden calf, and why would that be a significant god? Well, when one really reflects on it, perhaps we still worship cattle today. What do we call a booming market? A bull market. What do we call a profitable business? A cash cow.

Fig. 8. *The Adoration of the Golden Calf.* Before 1634 (oil on canvas) (see 205592-205594 for details), Poussin, Nicolas (1594-1665) National Gallery, London, UK/Bridgeman Images.

Cows represent wealth. Cows not only provide food, they provide business and enterprise. Cows give milk. Cows give meat. Cows can be sold. Are we susceptible to worshiping wealth, the fruit of our labor? The Israelites faltered in their faithfulness and fashioned an idol from the work of their hands. Our idol worship is not so different: we are prone to worship things that we make ourselves, such as money or fashion or prestige.

When Moses returns, he says, "What have you done?" He makes them grind the golden cow into fine dust and eat it, a fierce and awesome judgment on the people. Afterward, they build the tabernacle and the ark, and receive another set of tablets because Moses broke the first ones in anger.

CHAPTER 1 Exodus: The Founding of Israel 23

Promised Land

In fact, it did not take 40 years for the Israelites to go from Egypt to Canaan. Rather, it only took a few years for the Israelites to arrive at the promised land. This is the third major scene: when they arrived, they went in and spied on the land, but they saw that it was heavily populated, and that there were what they described as "giants" there.

Again, the people grumbled against Moses, his brother Aaron and the leaders of the Israelites. So the Lord told the Israelites that an entire generation of those who've come out of Egypt must die in the wilderness. They would have to raise up a new generation, one that had no Egypt in their system, who only knew the gracious provision of God. It was this generation that God would lead into the promised land. He would also take care of their enemies. It took 40 years to raise a new generation who did not have the slave mentality of dependence on Egypt. In other words, it took 40 years to get Egypt out of Israel. Only two men from the old generation, Joshua and Caleb, were allowed to enter.

As the creed continues: "and he brought us into this place and gave us this land, the land flowing with milk and honey." Joshua's name means "Yahweh saves." Through the leadership of Joshua, the Israelites would become a redeemed, delivered, and new people, created from bondage and the chaos of the wilderness to be the holy people of God. Joshua's leadership is remembered long after his time: for example, the name Jesus is the Greek form of Joshua. As the angel of the Lord revealed to Joseph concerning Mary, "She will bear a son, and you shall call his name Jesus, for he will save his people from their sins." (Matthew 1:21)

EXCURSUS: Validating the Exodus in the Historic Record

A challenging issue in developing a Christian worldview is establishing the historicity of the Bible. The parting of the Red Sea, plagues, manna, Mount Sinai—all of it sounds surreal and difficult to believe. For secular-minded people, much of it is indeed unbelievable.

The popular online encyclopedia, Wikipedia, describes the Exodus as "the founding myth of Israel."[00] It claims the Exodus narrative is not history and that "no archaeological evidence" has been found to support the historical accuracy of the Biblical story.[1]

In developing a Christian worldview, one must acknowledge multiple worldviews, which have many basic assumptions. Every verse, every story and every event in the Bible is scrutinized and questioned

---

excursus—(noun)
ex·cur·sus \ ik-`skər-səs
an appendix or digression that contains further exposition of some point or topic

Merriam-Webster Dictionary

and critiqued by unbelieving people. Every historical assertion the Bible makes is resisted and challenged. This resistance is based on history, fact, premise, ethical opinions and religious viewpoints.

Timeline and Archaeology

Part of the problem with the Exodus is that there are two different accounts of when it happened. One passage points to a later date for the events of the Exodus, around 1250 BC: *"Therefore they set taskmasters over them to afflict them with heavy burdens. They built for Pharaoh store cities, Pithom and Raamses." (Exodus 1:11)* The pharaohs for whom these cities would have been named, Ramesses I and Ramesses II, reigned back to back from the 1290s to 1213 BC.

Another passage indicates an earlier date around 1440 BC: *"In the four hundred and eightieth year after the people of Israel came out of the land of Egypt, in the fourth year of Solomon's reign over Israel, in the month of Ziv, which is the second month, he began to build the house of the LORD." (1 Kings 6:1)* The temple was built around 960 BC, which would put the approximate date of the Exodus at 1440 BC.

Manfred Bietak, a contemporary Austrian archaeologist, leads excavations taking place at Ramesses. If one were to ask him if there was any evidence that Israelites lived in the ancient city of Ramesses, his answer would be no. Bietak believes that the Bible dates the Exodus to approximately 1250 BC; and if this is true, then there could not have been any Israelites in the city during the time of the Exodus—exposing the entire story as no more than mythology.

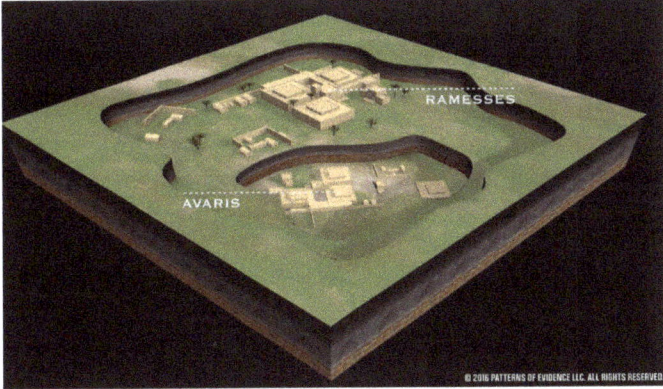

Fig. 9. *Map of Ramesses and Avaris.*

However, as Bietak and his crew were excavating the city of Ramesses, they discovered another, older city underneath it. That city, which was called Avaris, was populated by Canaanites who built tunnel houses in the Canaanite style and had very similar customs to the Israelites. A crucial discovery was a palace house that had 12 tombs. One of these tombs was a pyramid tomb, a prominent resting place for a non-Egyptian high authority. There also is a river at the site that to this day is called the Canal of Joseph, which strongly suggests that he is the high authority in the pyramid tomb (for whom the canal is named). The movie *Patterns of Evidence: Exodus* explains that there is indeed much evidence in favor of the historical veracity of the Exodus. If one adjusts the timeline to the earlier date in 1440 BC, then one can identify a pattern of evidence, at Avaris and elsewhere, that corroborates the arrival of the Israelites in Egypt, as well as their multiplication, their slavery, their judgment on Egypt, their Exodus and their conquest.

Fig. 10. *Timeline.* NEEDS ATTRIBUTION.

Educated readers of the scriptures and educated Christians must have a healthy dose of skepticism regarding the historical claims of skeptics. A single detail, such as the date of an event, can make the difference between a complete lack of archaeological evidence and a clear pattern of evidence, and this should not be forgotten as one reads secular scholars claim that no proof exists that events in the Bible actually happened.

APPLICATION OF THE EXODUS TO JESUS AND THE CHURCH

Throughout Exodus, the author asserts two important theological arguments. The first argument is that there is a cosmic battle raging for the souls of humanity. Yahweh is contending for the hearts and souls of his people against the cruel pharaoh, who believes that their hearts and souls belong to him. The Exodus, especially the Passover, is a sign of God's redemptive action. The blood put on the doorposts and lintels is the price paid for the children of Israel. When the Hebrews, generations later, would recount the story and make their offerings to God, their children might ask why the Passover is important. Their fathers' answers would be that the rites were an act of gratitude, for the Lord had bought them from slavery and called them to be his own people.

Exodus is about God's deliverance from bondage and tyranny. The Exodus provides Christians with the theology of God's guidance and provision. In addition, it tells us how his people received his grace and sanctification in their lives through his word and his love—which is a precursor to the grace and sanctification that we have received from Jesus Christ.

> **Theology of the Exodus:**
>
> *Cosmic Battle for the Souls of Humanity*
>
> *God's Redemption*
>
> *God's Deliverance*
>
> *God's Guidance and Provision*
>
> *Grace and Sanctification*

The second argument is that there is only one God. The so-called gods of other nations and tribes are utterly irrelevant and powerless, and Yahweh is the great God and warrior. Not even the pharaoh, arguably the most powerful ruler of his day, could withstand the might of the Lord. Though the forces of evil may appear mighty and overwhelming in our world today, they will not prevail, for God reigns as he did in the book of Exodus.

Lord's Supper, Cross and Resurrection

As one gave a tithe in offering, the creedal retelling of the Exodus would focus the heart and mind with a continuous reminder of God's redemption and deliverance of the Israelites. It acknowledges that every good gift comes from the powerfully gracious hand of God, and that the work of our hands and the fruit of our labor are not gods, but gifts that should continually remind us of the one true God who gave them to us.

> **Exodus to Jesus and the Church:**
> *Passover to Jesus' Last Supper*
> *New Exodus to The Cross and Resurrection*
> *Christian Life: Redemption and Deliverance*

In the same way, the annual celebration of the Passover meal of bread and wine would recollect God's gracious provision and deliverance from bondage. During the season of Passover, Jesus takes the bread and wine at his last supper and connects it to his own death and resurrection by calling the meal his body and blood. The cross is the true Passover offering. As Paul said in 1 Corinthians, through Jesus Christ, our Passover has been sacrificed for us. In the Eucharist, we remind ourselves of Paul's teaching when we proclaim, *"Christ our Passover is sacrificed for us; therefore let us keep the feast."*

This is how the Passover of the Lord, and the Exodus that gives to us an understanding of its power, is remembered every Sunday in our lives as Christians.

Justification and Sanctification

The Exodus is the central act of the Old Testament, and it shapes our understanding of much of Christian theology as we consider its application in our own lives. God is a gracious God who rescues us from the bondage of sin and evil. He has fought the cosmic battles against Satan and all the spiritual forces of evil. In the end, he will liberate us from a life of corruption and evil to a Sabbath rest in the promised land of his son, Jesus Christ.

CHAPTER 1 NOTES:

CHAPTER 2
Name: The God of Abraham, Isaac and, Jacob

Objective: The maturing disciple of Jesus will understand how Yahweh's unique covenant relationship with Abraham will become the means of salvation for the problem of humanity.

In the first chapter, we looked at the book of Exodus from the redemptive historical perspective and argued that God's mighty act in redeeming Israel is central to understanding the Bible. In this chapter, we will go back and study Genesis, the first book of the Bible, with an emphasis on the *literary perspective*.

The *literary perspective* considers a particular book of the Bible as a literary unit, with its own writer, genre, and original audience. One can also consider secondary aspects, like the circumstances and historic context of the book. Genesis, for example, belongs to the narrative genre; this means that, in studying Genesis as a literary unit, the student should consider aspects specific to the narrative genre such as character development, plot, and literary structure.

Fig. 1. *The Creation of Adam.* Michelangelo. 1508-1512. Fresco. Sistine Chapel, Vatican/Bridgeman Images.

- *Who is Yahweh?*
- *What is the purpose of humanity?*
- *What is wrong with humanity?*
- *Who is this nation named Israel and what is their unique role?*
- *How did Israel get enslaved in Egypt in the first place?*

Genesis: The Beginning of It All

In attempting to understand God's covenant with Israel in Exodus many questions may come to one's mind: who is this God, Yahweh who has made his presence so powerfully known? Why did he choose Israel as His people? What does God have in mind for these people? While the Exodus is central in the formation of Israel, the answers to these questions can be found in Genesis.

We can discern three major narrative sections in the Book of Genesis. The story of God and humanity is in Chapters 1 through 11. Next, there are the stories of the patriarchs Abraham, Isaac, and Jacob in Chapters 12 through 36. Finally, we read the story of Joseph in Chapters 37-50.

THE RELATIONSHIP OF YAHWEH AND CREATION (GENESIS 1-11)

The story of God and humanity reveals Yahweh to us. Yahweh, or "I am," is the personal covenant name of God. He is the creator of all things, yet he has a special interest in mankind. He is a God who establishes order and expresses concern. He delights in his creation, declaring it good and very good. He is holy and created for us a special holy day, the Sabbath.

The Name of Yahweh

"At that time people began to call upon the name of the Lord."
(Genesis 4:26b)

"Then Moses said to God,
"If I come to the people of Israel and say to them,
'The God of your fathers has sent me to you,'
and they ask me, 'What is his name?' what shall I say to them?"
God said to Moses, "I AM WHO I AM."
And he said, "Say this to the people of Israel: 'I AM has sent me to you.'"

God also said to Moses, "Say this to the people of Israel:
'The Lord, the God of your fathers, the God of Abraham,
the God of Isaac, and the God of Jacob, has sent me to you.'
This is my name forever and thus I am to be remembered throughout all generations."
(Exodus 3:13-15)

Fig. 2. *Yod Hay Vav Hay.*

The creation narrative should be viewed primarily as a theological and poetic description of the beginning of the world, rather than as a scientific description. It also serves as a polemic against polytheism:

the creation stories of other contemporaneous religions described the world as a byproduct of actions and affairs of multiple pagan gods. Moses, the author, would have known these stories well: his privileged upbringing in the pharaoh's court helped to make him arguably the best-educated man of his day. Knowing that the Israelites needed to understand that there was only one true God, Moses ensured that Genesis is unique, and clearly distinct from other creation narratives. Unlike the pagan narratives, things like the sun, the moon, and the stars are not gods at all—they are creations of the one true God, Yahweh.

As Genesis tells us what God has created, it also takes care to show that God sees everything he creates as good. However, it also shows how man went astray by introducing to us the problem of evil.

The story of the seven days of creation is a literary prologue of redemptive history: in Genesis, we see the transition from Chaos to Sabbath rest; in Joshua, from wilderness to Promised Land; and in the Gospels, from sinner to new creation in Christ. The rule of God on Earth is mediated personally through the Messiah.

According to Genesis, God made man and woman from the "dust of the ground." By his breath, he granted them life. And in his "image and likeness" he created them. Because they are made to resemble the creator, they have a special dignity which sets them apart from the rest of God's creation.

By giving humans his image and likeness, God also gives them a charge to be good stewards of creation: they must be accountable for their actions, communicate with God and one another, bring about good in the world, use their power only in the name of that good, and care for their neighbors. When they do these things, humans reflect the glory of the creator.

When God declares that his creation is good, he does not mean that it is perfect; rather, he simply means that it is "suitable for the purposes of God." The Garden of Eden is not land that comes bearing fruit, it is land made to be tended. It is filled with possibilities and latent potential for the humans that will tend it. There are resources such as iron and gold in the ground waiting to be discovered. With the divine mandate to rule and fill the earth, humanity will press the story forward.

In later books, when God separates the waters of the Red Sea and the Jordan River, he reveals that his power can not only create humans, but also deliver them from their distress and lead them in to a new and promised Sabbath Rest. The new covenant sees these as types and symbols of a greater Sabbath Rest found in an intimate relationship with Jesus Christ.

---

polemic—(noun)
po·lem·ic \ pə-ˈle-mik
a: an aggressive attack on or refutation of the opinions or principles of another; b: the art or practice of disputation or controversy

Merriam-Webster Dictionary

"For if Joshua had given them rest,
God would not have spoken of another day later on.
So then, there remains a Sabbath rest for the people of God,
for whoever has entered God's rest
has also rested from his works as God did from his.
Let us therefore strive to enter that rest,
so that no one may fall by the same sort of disobedience."
(Hebrews 4:8-11)

HUMANITY AND THE FALL: (Genesis 1-3)

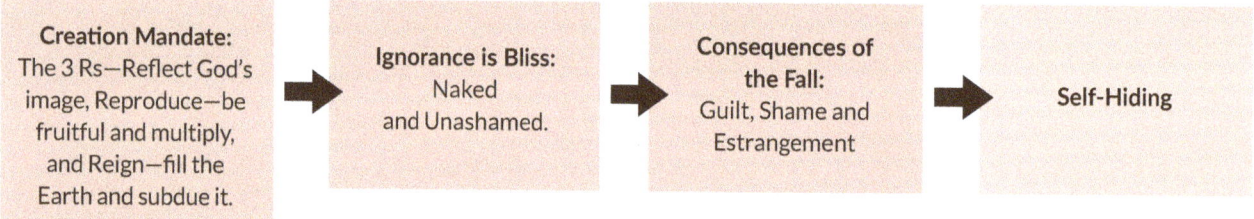

Creation Mandate: The 3 Rs—Reflect God's image, Reproduce—be fruitful and multiply, and Reign—fill the Earth and subdue it. → **Ignorance is Bliss:** Naked and Unashamed. → **Consequences of the Fall:** Guilt, Shame and Estrangement → **Self-Hiding**

Adam and Eve

The first covenant between God and man appears in the book of Genesis. God creates Adam and Eve, and personally directs them to reflect his image, reproduce with each other, and reign over the Earth.

However, after the fall, the relationship between God and humanity is forever changed. Before Adam and Eve ate the fruit of the tree of the knowledge of good and evil, they lived in blissful ignorance. But evil and sin are introduced into the creation mandate through their disobedience to God, who had specifically warned them not to eat from that tree. Because of the corruption of humanity, Adam and Eve immediately begin to struggle with fear, shame, self-hiding, estrangement and death.

Sin only expresses itself in even more extreme ways with Adam and Eve's descendants. Their son, Cain, commits the first murder against his own brother, Abel. To this day, individual sin seeks to control and manipulate human beings through daily temptation. Since we are too weak to resist on our own, and enjoy indulging ourselves too much, we find ourselves in bondage to sin.

In addition to being slaves, we find that we are victims to sin in other ways as well. The promise of the *proto-evangelium* in Genesis 3:15 is

Fig. 4. *Adam and Eve.* Tiziano, Vecellio. C. 1550. Oil on canvas. Museo del Prado, Madrid/Bridgeman Images.

that evil would one day be crushed under the feet of a human deliverer—but not without cost. (A *proto-evangelium* is literally the first Gospel—it is a first glimpse at the message of salvation.) The eve's child will one day crush the evil serpent; however, in doing so, the child of eve will be wounded.

"The LORD God said to the serpent,
'Because you have done this,
cursed are you above all livestock
and above all beasts of the field;
on your belly you shall go,
and dust you shall eat all the days of your life.
I will put enmity between you and the woman,
and between your offspring and her offspring;
he shall bruise your head
and you shall bruise his heel.'"
(Genesis 3:14-15)

Sin and Consequences:
Guilt

Shame

Fear

Estrangement

Actions

Bondage

Victims

Collusion

Sorrow

Rage

Death

The Toledot Formula

The *Toledot Formula* is a recurring phrase in Genesis that signals that the narrative is changing its focus onto a new character. Literally, *todelot* means "This is the account of" in Hebrew. It is used 10 times in Genesis: five times from Adam to Abraham, and five times from Abraham to Israel in Egypt.

The Toledot Formula reveals the literary framework of the book: by linking all of the major figures with a common introduction, it underscores the fact that Israel, through Adam, has a common ancestry with all the nations of the world. Because of this, all nations also share a common history of grace, rebellion, and revolution. At the same time, by highlighting specific individuals and families, the Toledot structure reminds us that God has graciously elected particular people and particular families to take part in the gradual redemption of the entire human race.

Toledot Formula of Generations:

| Adam | All of Humanity | Noah | Shem | Abram | Isaac | Jacob | 12 Tribes |

Covenant with Noah

God's second covenant, with Noah, occurs as a result of humanity's near-complete corruption. Man's sinfulness is contrasted with God's judgment, salvation, covenant, and promise.

Fig. 5. *The Flood.* Carracci, Antonio. 1616-1618. Oil on canvas. Musée du Louvre, Paris.

"The Lord saw that the wickedness of man was great in the earth, and that every intention of the thoughts of his heart was only evil continually.

And the Lord regretted that he had made man on the earth, and it grieved him to his heart."
(Genesis 6:5-6)

Because Noah alone of all men is good, God decides to make him the father of mankind after he floods the earth and kills all living things not on the ark. The flood ends with a divine promise, the covenant of the bow in the clouds. God makes a promise of judgment against himself as he points his war bow to the heavens:

Fig. 6. *Noah Gives Thanks for Deliverance.* Morelli, Domenico. 1901. Oil on canvas. NEEDS ATTRIBUTION.]

"I have set my bow in the cloud,
and it shall be a sign of the covenant between me and the earth.
When I bring clouds over the earth and the bow is seen in the clouds,

I will remember my covenant that is between me and youand
every living creature of all flesh.
And the waters shall never again become a flood to destroy all flesh."
(Genesis 9:13-15)

The Tower of Babel

Sin, of course, can be corporate as well as individual. When multiple people work together towards a common goal, they can achieve it more effectively, and on a greater scale, than any one person could achieve on his own. Unfortunately, this is true both when they work for good and when they work for evil.

The construction of the Tower of Babel introduces the power of sin as a cooperative, collective enterprise. The people of the world decide to make a name for themselves, by their own power—without God. Human rebellion against the rule of God reaches a climax in the Tower of Babel.

Fig. 7. Bruegel, Pieter the Elder. *The Tower of Babel.* 1563. Oil on panel. Kunsthistorisches Museum, Vienna/Bridgeman Images.

"Then they said, 'Come, let us build ourselves a city and a tower with its top in the heavens, and let us make a name for ourselves, lest we be dispersed over the face of the whole earth.' And the Lord came down to see the city and the tower, which the children of man had built."
(Genesis 11:4-5)

Something very wrong has happened to creation over the course of several generations. God's declaration, "Let us make man" led to humanity declaring, "Let us make a name for ourselves." God's command for man to fill the entire earth instead became the concentration and consolidation of the people within Babel. A family in fellowship with God became a community in rebellion, and a world of harmony became a world of confusion.

But God's blessing on humans persists even in their rebellion. After God puts an end to the rebellion, he chooses a single man to aid in the redemption of humanity: Abraham.

THE RELATIONSHIP OF YAHWEH AND ISRAEL
(Genesis 12-36)

Covenant with Abraham

In Genesis 12, God makes a new covenant (known as the *Abrahamic Covenant*) with his servant Abraham, which is then inherited by his son Isaac and his grandson Jacob. God's grace is not new, for God showed grace to Noah and his descendants in promising never to flood the Earth again. What is new is the expression of *redemptive* grace in a covenant. God's promises to Abraham are graciously and freely given, and humanity is renewed through Abraham and his seed.

- Why is Israel so important to Yahweh?

- Why is Yahweh helping them?

- Aren't there other people who need deliverance?

- How will Yahweh restore humanity?

*"Now the Lord said to Abram,
'Go from your country and your kindred and your father's house
to the land that I will show you.
And I will make of you a great nation,
and I will bless you and make your name great,
so that you will be a blessing.
I will bless those who bless you,
and him who dishonors you I will curse,
and in you all the families of the earth shall be blessed.' ...*

*When they came to the land of Canaan,
Abram passed through the land to the place at Shechem,
to the oak of Moreh.
At that time the Canaanites were in the land.
Then the Lord appeared to Abram and said,
'To your offspring I will give this land.'"*
(Genesis 12:1-3, 5b-7)

Fig. 8. Brunelleschi, Filippo. *Sacrifice of Isaac.* 1401. Bronze relief. Museo Nazionale del Bargello, Florence/Bridgeman Images.

But God does not focus solely on Abraham; he includes other nations, kings, and lands in his plan. Genesis explores Israel's relationship with other nations and tribes. The Israelites, ever conscious of their special relationship with God, set themselves apart from all others through circumcision. Some are friends and cousins of Abraham, and some are completely corrupt and hostile to him and his wife. Some of them Abraham will fight, and some of them, such as Sodom and Gomorrah, God himself will fight.

God promises Abraham a homeland, declaring that, if he were to break his promise, Yahweh would walk between sacrificed animals as a sign of judgment.

God teaches faith, hope, and patience to Abraham and his family though trials and testing. And the family serves as a unique means for his promises and covenants to be transmitted.

Abraham and Jacob, in particular, experience a world drowning in alienation, anguish, pain, evil, and death. They are tested, and they remain steadfast in faith even when called upon to sacrifice that which is dear. Their perseverance produces faith, hope and love in the lives of the entire family, and in this way, the patriarchs model a true life of faith in this world.

"And the angel of the LORD called to Abraham a second time from heaven and said,
'By myself I have sworn, declares the LORD,
because you have done this and have not withheld your son, your only son,
I will surely bless you, and I will surely multiply your offspring
as the stars of heaven and as the sand that is on the seashore.
And your offspring shall possess the gate of his enemies,
and in your offspring shall all the nations of the earth be blessed,
because you have obeyed my voice.'"
(Genesis 22:15-18)

"Then he said, 'Your name shall no longer be called Jacob, but Israel, for you have striven with God and with men, and have prevailed.'"
(Genesis 32:28)

God makes four promises to the patriarchs: first, he promises them a multitude of offspring; second, he promises them a land for their descendants; third, he promises them his blessings of presence, protection, and guidance to the patriarchs; and finally, he promises the same blessings to the nations. These promises and covenants are ultimately and fully accomplished in Jesus Christ, who is rightly called "the hope of the nations."

Fig. 9. Caravaggio. *The Sacrifice of Isaac.* 1601-1602. Oil on canvas. Galleria degli Uffizi, Florence/ Bridgeman Images.

THE RELATIONSHIP OF ISRAEL AND EGYPT (Genesis 37-50)

When Joseph's brothers sold him into slavery in Egypt, little did they know that the Israelites had at that moment sold themselves into the same slavery! Through sin, we sell ourselves into bondage. The desire to harm others, no matter how subtle, is in the heart of every human being, and is the root of such sins as extortion, lust, lies, corruption, family abuse, and murder. When we commit these sins against our neighbors, we will experience many consequences: guilt, shame, estrangement, grief, sorrow, and victimhood. Even though the children of Abraham are to be the means of salvation to the world, they themselves are in need of the same deliverance from the very same sin.

• How did the Israelites get to Egypt in the first place?

Fig. 11. Ferenczy, Károly. *Joseph Sold into Slavery by his Brothers.* 1900. Oil on canvas. Magyar Nemzeti Galéria, Budapest.

Throughout the story of Joseph, the author emphasizes the importance of cloaks. Joseph bears three garments that can reveal either the honor or shame of a person. The first cloak is the "robe of many colors," which shows both Joseph's high status and the intense love of his father Jacob, and makes Joseph the object of the scorn and jealousy of his brothers. Joseph is literally stripped of this dignity when his brothers sell him and dip the cloak in an animal's blood in order to convince Jacob that his favorite son has died a gruesome death.

Joseph's second cloak is in Chapter 39. The wife of his master Potiphar takes a liking to him and attempts to seduce him. When she grabs Joseph's cloak, he shows integrity by "leaving his garment in her hand and fleeing." However, Potiphar's wife, angry and humiliated, uses the garment as false evidence that Joseph had raped her. Potiphar, believing his wife, imprisons his slave, and the cloak, which should be a sign of integrity, instead becomes an object of shame.

Joseph receives the third cloak from the pharaoh, after "wisely" interpreting the ruler's dream with the seven fat cows and the seven lean cows. This robe of nobility symbolizes the status to which God elevates and blesses Joseph: from humiliation as a discarded brother, slave and prisoner to honor as a trusted adviser of the pharaoh.

The story of Joseph, and his cloaks, show us that though humans may strip a person of his earthly reputation and status by force and deception, the Lord bestows heavenly reputation and status upon that person that cannot be taken away from him.

We also can learn much about Joseph's brother Judah through his clothes and accessories: just as cloaks are symbols of status, integrity, and disgrace for Joseph, ring and scepter serve to symbolize royal status and personal disgrace for Judah. Despite Judah's evil intent and Joseph's faithfulness to God, it is Judah's descendant, not Joseph's, who will eventually become the King of Israel (Genesis 49:8-12). However, before this can happen, Judah must learn humility and self-control in his leadership.

His scepter, or staff, is both his glory and his downfall. Judah's own sin led him to put up the signet ring and the staff of his rule as collateral for his pledge to a "prostitute," his daughter-in-law Tamar. Later, Judah would pledge his own life as collateral for his brother Benjamin and show the maturity of a true leader.

Fig. 12. Lievens, Jan. *Jacob Receiving the Bloody Tunic of Joseph.* c. 1640s. Oil on canvas. Private Collection.

Despite her past, Tamar would become the matriarch of the Messiah, the one to whom the "obedience of the nations" belongs. In Matthew 1:2-3, Judah, Tamar, and their son Perez figure prominently in the genealogy of Jesus.

Fig. 16. Tiepolo, Giovanni Battista. *Joseph Receiving Pharaoh's Ring.* c. 1733-1735. Oil on canvas. Dulwich Picture Gallery, London.

"As for you, you meant evil against me,
but God meant it for good,
to bring it about that many people should be kept alive,
as they are today."
(Genesis 50:20)

Thankfully for us, the human intention for evil is outweighed by the divine intention for good. Though evil begets only evil, God, with his awesome power, uses the thoroughly evil actions of Joseph's brothers and of Israel to accomplish his good plan of salvation. Joseph, after everything that his brothers did to him, unexpectedly gains absolute power over their lives; and yet, his heart is moved to show them nothing but compassion and love. The jealousy and hatred of the brothers toward Joseph is repaid with humility and servitude.

When Judah pledges to sacrifice his own life in exchange for the life of his brother Benjamin, Joseph "could not control himself." His emotions flooded in tears of love and forgiveness for his family. Joseph is reconciled to the family, and Judah shows the character of a true king: one who will lay down his own life for that of his people.

However, the consequences of the brothers' sin remain: in their desperation, they find that they and their descendants are slaves to Egypt. Though Joseph is given pre-eminence over Israel and Egypt for his wisdom and response to the vision of God, eventually all of Israel will sell their freedom and inheritance to the pharaoh for their daily bread. While such an exchange is a temporary blessing, it will prove a cruel bondage for the Israelites, especially when a pharaoh who knows nothing of Joseph's service to Egypt rises to power.

God's promise of the great nation that will ultimately bless all nations occurs in the wider context of the universal kingdom of the world. God looks after both his special kingdom of Israel and his global kingdom. He speaks and reveals his sovereign will to Joseph and to the pharaoh in dreams. God's universal dominion over the entire world provides food for the preservation of his special unique kingdom. And the special kingdom offers to the rest of the world the prophetic voice of God and the mediation of his covenant blessings.

God's plan involves other nations in the global kingdom interacting with Israel. Without Egypt, Israel would have starved; without Israel, Egypt would have starved from a famine of God's revealed word.

Joseph, like Daniel and others in the story arc of redemptive history, must learn how to be in the world but not of it—to integrate with the earth and serve the universal kingdom without compromise. God can and will continue to preserve and bless the faithful remnant among his people, even in the midst of exile.

The Bible is full of paradoxes. One of the most striking ones is that, even though its people are at war with the nations that rebel against God's rule, the nation of Israel will ultimately be a blessing to those same nations. When God promises to Abraham that in him "all the families of the earth shall be blessed" (Genesis 12:3), he means that they will be blessed through his descendants, and especially through Jesus, who will one day bring the hope of salvation to the entire world.

God's purpose in revealing his call to a particular people and family was to fulfill a divine plan. Abraham was called to leave one land and go instead to a land of God's provision. God tests the faith of his chosen people through their response to his revelation and calling, and Genesis, again and again, shows to us that tests, struggles and temptations in part serve to prove the genuineness of that faithful response.

The responses of the patriarchs set the example for faith and for trusting in God's promises, and provide positive and negative examples of how the people of God can dwell in a world alienated from its creator.

---

paradox—(noun)
par·a·dox \ per-ə-däks, pa-rə-
a statement that is seemingly contradictory or opposed to common sense and yet is perhaps true

Merriam-Webster Dictionary

We See the Providence of God

Ultimately, the purpose of Genesis was to teach the Israelites that God's plan for them was to leave Egypt and rule over Canaan. Yahweh is a God who not only makes promises, but also fulfills them.

Knowledge of good and evil will come to mean wisdom for those humans who are willing to learn. This wisdom comes from knowing the deepest and most hidden intentions of the human heart and understanding that the intention of God's heart is to love humanity. Through Abraham, his heirs, and particularly Judah, a king will be born who will save and bless all the nations of the world through his most gracious rule.

"The scepter shall not depart from Judah,
nor the ruler's staff from between his feet,
until tribute comes to him;
and to him shall be the obedience of the peoples."
(Genesis 49:10)

> **Theological Considerations:**
>
> *Yahweh is the one true God, creator of all things*
>
> *Humanity is corrupt.*
>
> *Annihilating judgment is not the answer, but what is?*
>
> *Yahweh has made covenant with Abraham, Isaac and Jacob—to bless the nations*
>
> *Israel lacks integrity, is divided and corrupt, selling itself into slavery*

CHAPTER 2 NOTES:

CHAPTER 3
Torah: The Law of Moses

Objective: The maturing disciple of Jesus Christ will understand the fundamental role of the Law of Moses (the Torah) as the engine of the Old Covenant that drives Israel to become a great nation bring God's salvation and blessing to the world.

From a literary perspective, the covenant in the book of Deuteronomy follows a convention similar to ancient Near Eastern covenant treaties between the kings and subjects of nations. The difference is that, unlike those earthly covenants, it is a covenant between Yahweh and his people. The importance of Deuteronomy in the larger canon of Scripture cannot be overstated: just as the Constitution guides the history of the United States, so Deuteronomy serves as the governing document, or canonical engine, for the nation of Israel. A canonical perspective is one in which the various books of the Old Testament are analyzed in relationship to one another. Deuteronomy is key to understanding the interrelationships of all of the Old Testament books.

Deuteronomy means "second law" in Greek. However, a more accurate translation is "copy" (Deuteronomy 17:18), where the king is told to make a copy of the law and carry it with him, to remind himself that everyone lives under it.

OUTLINE OF DEUTERONOMY: How Does God Make a Covenant with a Nation?

In the book of Genesis, we learn that because of Adam and Eve's disobedience to God, all human beings fell into sin. This sin invades every aspect of our lives, and we resist it with great difficulty because we are predisposed to it. Since the Fall, it has always been a part of who we are.

From Genesis, we also learn how sin, when left unchecked, can bring about incredibly destructive consequences for humanity. From Cain's

Deuteronomy Outline:

Preamble (1:1-4)

Historic Prologue (1:5-4:43)

Commandments (4:44-26:19)

Blessings and Curses (27-30)

Succession (31-34)

murder of his brother Abel to the selling of Joseph into slavery, the message of Genesis is that human beings, when given the opportunity, love to rebel against God. To make matters worse, the innate nature of sin means that it is transmitted from generation to generation. It does not die when a sinful generation dies; instead, it multiplies with human beings.

Fig. 1. Bruegel, Pieter the Elder. *The Tower of Babel.* 1563. Oil on panel. Kunsthistorisches Museum, Vienna/Bridgeman Images.

What, then, is God to do about those who reject his authority? He has two options: the more obvious one is, of course, simply to get rid of nearly all human beings, preserving only the most righteous among them. The story of the flood illustrates why this will not work: even when God brings humanity down to a single family, headed by the righteous and faithful Noah, we see that his descendants remain carriers of sin. Even the most righteous man in the world is afflicted, and sin continues to spread with the generations that came after Noah.

What, then, is the other option? It begins with a man named Abraham. Through this faithful but flawed man, God ordains one family who will grow into the nation of Israel. Over many centuries, God uses this nation to redeem the entire world. The last story of Genesis, about Joseph's time in Egypt, not only explains how the Israelites ended up in Egypt, but also how, because of their own sins, sold themselves into slavery and bondage. It is why we speak of "the sin that enslaves us:" it promises us freedom from God and then delivers us to the cruel Prince of the World.

God's Providence

However, the Lord does not forget the plight of his people. He uses that plight in order to manifest his power and mercy in mighty acts of judgement, redemption and deliverance. Joseph showed mercy to his brothers when, in the midst of a terrible famine, they came to him begging and pleading for food and provision.

Thankfully for Joseph's brothers, the Lord had given power directly to Joseph. He had access to the food and provisions that they sought. And though he had the opportunity to avenge the injustice they had done to him, Joseph chose instead to tell them in Genesis 50:20 that what they had meant for evil, God had meant for good, so that thousands of people; through Joseph, could be delivered from famine.

That little verse—What you meant for evil, God meant for good—goes a long way toward explaining everything that happens in the Bible. God's greatest act of love, the death of his son on the cross for the sins of the world, is the ultimate expression of God using evil human intentions and actions to accomplish his good purposes.

The people of Jerusalem, in their fear and anger, crucify the Lord and Savior of the world—who is without any sin, and thus for whom any punishment is not only unjust, but unjustifiable. All of the authorities—the powers of humanity, the highest powers, the Roman Empire—are crucifying Jesus. The *very people of God* are crucifying Jesus. As they crucify him, he is compelled to cry out, "Father, forgive them, for they know not what they do." And yet, even this would become the very means by which God would make good on all of his promises. We meant it for evil, but he meant it for good.

"As for you, you meant evil against me,
but God meant it for good,
to bring it about that many people should be kept alive,
as they are today."
(Genesis 50:20)

Fig. 2. Tiepolo, Giovanni Battista. *Joseph Receiving Pharaoh's Ring.* c. 1733-1735. Oil on canvas. Dulwich Picture Gallery, London.

God's Plan

Genesis tells us that Yahweh is the one true creator. He is the only God, who therefore has a relationship with all human beings even if they do not know him yet. But these humans, and by extension the rest of creation, are corrupt, and it is clear to God that annihilating judgment is not the way to bring his creation back into faithfulness. He could, in theory, remove the corruption by removing humanity. But that would be throwing out the baby with the bathwater! Rather, God has something far better in mind.

What is his plan? It involves the patriarchs: God made a covenant with Abraham, Isaac and Jacob. Through that covenant, they became instruments to bless the peoples of this world. Even though they were the means through which God would save the world, the nation Israel, like all others, continued to struggle with the problem of sin.

"'I will never again curse the ground because of man,
for the intention of man's heart is evil from his youth.'"
(Genesis 8:21)

Theological Considerations:

Yahweh is the one true God, creator of all things

Humanity is corrupt.

Annihilating judgment is not the answer, but what is?

Yahweh has made covenant with Abraham, Isaac and Jacob—to bless the nations

Israel lacks integrity, is divided and corrupt, selling itself into slavery

Six Covenants of the Old Testament

1 Adam (Genesis 1-3)	2 Noah (Genesis 8)	3 Abraham (Genesis 12, 15)	4 Moses (Deuteronomy)	5 David (2 Samuel 7)	6 New Covenant (Jeremiah 31)

There are six covenants in the Old Testament. The first covenant is with Adam, the creation mandate. It involves three Rs: *Reflect* God's image, *Reproduce*—be fruitful and multiply—and *Reign*–fill the Earth and subdue it.

The second covenant is with Noah: God promises never again to annihilate the world through overwhelming flood and puts his bow—a rainbow—in the clouds.

The third covenant, with Abraham, comprises the seven "I Wills," which include: *I will make your name great. I will make you a great nation. I will bless all the nations of the world through you. I will give you this land.*

The fourth covenant is with Israel through Moses. The fifth covenant is with David, a ministry of kingly rule and everlasting throne. And finally, the new covenant, through Jesus, is also mentioned in the Old Testament.

COVENANT: The Basis of Prophetic Lawsuit and Promise

In the ancient Near East, treaties and covenants were an essential part of the culture. There were several kinds of covenants: the simplest kind was made between two individuals. The two people would chop animals in half, and then the two parties would walk between the carcasses. The splitting of the animals' bodies served as a message: if the covenant was broken, then the individuals should be split as well (see Jeremiah 34:18-20). This is where the phrase "cutting a deal" originates. The covenant will cut you off if you break it; it will curse you.

Covenants Between Two People

Abraham made this kind of covenant with God. Abraham wanted to be sure that God would keep his promises; in response, God told Abraham: "Very well. I will behave like a man, and we will cut a deal. I want you to prepare the carcasses, cut them all in half, and line them up."

[Fig. 3. Slide 6. NEEDS ATTRIBUTION.]

However, when Abraham prepared the carcasses, God did not appear. Birds of prey circled around the carcasses and Abraham attempted to chase them away. Exhausted, he fell asleep. When he awoke, he had a vision of a smoking fire pot passing through the middle of the carcasses. This fire pot was, in fact, the Lord, who guaranteed the land of Canaan to Abraham's descendants:

"And he said to him,
'I am the LORD who brought you out from Ur of the Chaldeans
to give you this land to possess.'
But he said, 'O LORD God, how am I to know that I shall possess it?'
He said to him, 'Bring me a heifer three years old, a female goat three years old,
a ram three years old, a turtledove and a young pigeon.'
And he brought him all these,
cut them in half, and laid each half over against the other.
But he did not cut the birds in half.
And when birds of prey came down on the carcasses, Abram drove them away.
As the sun was going down, a deep sleep fell on Abram.
And behold, dreadful and great darkness fell upon him.
Then the Lord said to Abram, 'Know for certain that your offspring will be sojourners
in a land that is not theirs and will be servants there,
and they will be afflicted for four hundred years.
But I will bring judgment on the nation that they serve,
and afterward they shall come out with great possessions.
As for you, you shall go to your fathers in peace; you shall be buried in a good old age.
And they shall come back here in the fourth generation,
for the iniquities of the Amorites is not yet complete.'

When the sun had gone down and it was dark,
behold, a smoking fire pot and a flaming torch passed between these pieces.
On that day the Lord made a covenant with Abram, saying,
'To your offspring I give this land, from the river of Egypt to the great river,
the river Euphrates, the land of the Kenites, the Kenizzites,
the Kadmonites, the Hittites, the Perizzites, the Rephaim,
the Amorites, the Canaanites, the Girgashites and the Jebusites."
(Genesis 15:7-21)

In contrast to a typical covenant, in which both men walked between the body parts together, God walked between the carcasses alone. Abraham did not have to walk between the carcasses and accept the punishment for failure; God did that on his behalf. All of the downside, all of the risk in the covenant, is assumed by God. This was great news for Abraham, who, because of sin, would not be able to keep up his end of the covenant. But God, who is always faithful to his promises, will uphold the entire covenant on his own.

Covenants Between a King and His Subjects

Another important kind of covenant was the covenant between a king and his subjects. The customs were quite different from a covenant between two equal individuals, and we can gain many insights by examining ancient Near Eastern treaties of this kind. The best-preserved examples of these ancient treaties have been discovered on Cuneiform tablets from the Hittite empire of 1700-1200 BC.

God mentions the Hittites in his covenant with Abraham. Hittite royal treaties, also known as suzerain-vassal treaties, were between two unequal parties, the suzerain (or master) and the vassal (or servant). They date back to the days of Moses and the Israelites. Suzerain-vassal treaties were very complex and intricate documents, containing a preamble, historic prologues, stipulations, ratification ceremonies, divine witnesses, blessings and curses, and succession.

When the Hittite king conquered other tribes or nations, he would make a covenant with them in order to create order and to make his dominance over them official. The preamble to the covenant made it very clear: he was their suzerain, or sovereign, and they were his vassals, or subjects.

Next, the king would recount a historic prologue of his benevolent rule: the vassals were in chaotic disarray in his absence. When he arrived, he began to fight their battles for them; he offered them much-needed protection from their dangerous world; in times of famine, he provided them with the food he had stored. His subjects were not to forget the king's kindness; they were to reward him with their obedience and loyalty.

Then came the stipulations and the ratification. The king would lay down laws for his vassal to observe. To reinforce these laws, the king's representatives would conduct annual ceremonies to ratify them by reading them out loud to the people.

After this, the king would call upon either his gods or the gods of

Ancient Near-Eastern Hittite Suzerain-Vassal Treaties Listed:

Preamble

Historical Prologue

Stipulations

Ratification

Divine Witness

Blessings and Curses

Succession

the vassal as witnesses to the covenant. What greater authority than a god, or gods, to provide legitimacy to such a covenant, especially after a brutal conquest?

The blessings and curses associated with the covenant followed the witness. In essence, the blessings claim that if the vassal people fulfills its end of the deal, then they would live in peace and prosperity, in harmony with their ruler. The curses, however, warn that the consequences of breaking the covenant were severe: the king would not only withdraw his provision and protection, but may even send his armies into their land, pillage their cities, and bring about many other severe judgments.

Finally, the king wanted to ensure that the treaty would not expire upon his own death. He wrote a section concerning succession to assert that his descendants would have legal claim to rule over the vassals and insure the covenant with their descendants.

Covenants Between God and His People

The literary structure of the book of Deuteronomy follows the form of one of these ancient Near Eastern treaties, with the crucial distinction that it was not written between a human king and his subjects. It was not a covenant between Moses, as if he were a king, and the Israelites, as if they were his subjects; Moses did not claim that he would be the one who led them out of the wilderness, and that the Israelites owned him their allegiance. It did assert that God had granted Moses authority, but only as the scribe and ambassador of the covenant between God and his people. God was the suzerain, and the Israelites (including Moses) were the vassals.

The Divine Covenant Treaty:
Israel and Yahweh

The photograph to the right shows the Column of Soleb. It dates back to the 14th century B.C. The Egyptian king Amenophis II made the column as a depiction of the surrounding nations as prisoners of Egypt. The man on it, who is not an Egyptian, has his arms tied behind his back. Sometimes, the hieroglyphics name the geographic location of the group represented. But this column translates to "the Shasus of Yahweh," wanderers of Yahweh. They are not identified by a place or a city-state, as the groups on the other columns are. Instead, these people are identified primarily by their relationship with their God. This is the oldest archaeological discovery where the name Yahweh is used—in Egyptian hieroglyphics!

Deuteronomy first names the parties. The covenant was between Yahweh, the one true God of Israel (and, according to Genesis, the one true God of the world), and the nation of Israel.

Fig. 4. *The Shasus of Yahweh* (back Column of Soleb (modern-day Sudan). 14th Century B.C. (dating from the time of Amenophis III 1391-1353 B.C.

The first four chapters in Deuteronomy act as an historic prologue, describing God's acts of redemption and multiple battles in which the Israelites overcome enemies with God's help. These chapters also recount when God graciously and abundantly provided for the Israelites, especially in the wilderness.

Then come the stipulations: the Ten Commandments function as a summary of all of God's laws.

And Moses summoned all Israel and said to them, "Hear, O Israel, the statutes and the rules that I speak in your hearing today, and you shall learn them and be careful to do them. The LORD our God made a covenant with us in Horeb. Not with our fathers did the LORD make this covenant, but with us, who are all of us here alive today.
(Deuteronomy 5:1-4)

Israel needed guidance and direction from God, because its people were both clueless and corrupted. They were prone to worship other gods, like the golden calf. They had been captive in Egypt for generations and knew little other than Egyptian morality, Egyptian law, and Egyptian practices. Deuteronomy thus provided the framework and the direction that the Israelites need.

But what is the importance of Moses' going up Mount Sinai to receive the law? Why can he not simply receive it in the presence of the other Israelites?

It is because God, the most fearsome being of all, was the source of Moses' authority and the commandments' authority. Did these commandments come from Moses? Were they something that humans made up? Not according to Deuteronomy: the Israelites had already heard God tell them the Ten Commandments directly—and it was terrifying. Because they feared continuing to hear God's voice, they sent Moses as their mediator and God agreed to relay his laws through Moses.

"While I stood between the LORD and you at that time,
to declare to you the word of the LORD.
For you were afraid because of the fire,
and you did not go up into the mountain."
(Deuteronomy 5:5)

The Ten Commandments

The Lord begins to list the commandments: *"I am the LORD your God, who brought you out of the land of Egypt, out of the house of slavery. You shall have no other gods but for me. You shall not make for yourself an idol, whether in the form of anything that is in heaven above or in the earth beneath or is in the water below the earth. You shall not bow down to them or worship them, for I, the LORD your God, am a jealous God, punishing children for the iniquity of their parents to the third and fourth generation of those who reject me but showing steadfast love to thousands of those who love me." (Deuteronomy 5:6-10).*

LORD is capitalized when it refers to God's distinctive personal name: **Yahweh**

The two great commandments given to us by Jesus in the Gospels are summaries of the Ten Commandments. In traditional church services, these are often recited: we start with the first one, "Love the Lord your God with all your heart, mind, soul and strength." This comes from the *Shema*. *Shema* means "hear." *"Hear, O Israel: the LORD our God, the LORD is one. You shall love the LORD your God with all your heart and with all your soul and with all your might" (Deuteronomy 6:4).* The second commandment is very much like it; You shall love your neighbor as yourself. *"On these two commandments," Jesus said, "depend all the Law and the Prophets" (Matthew 22:40).*

Thus, the Ten Commandments hang on those two commandments. The first being to love the Lord. The second being to love your neighbor. The first four commandments have to do with our relationship with God. The last six of the commandments have to do with relationships horizontally, with other people—honoring parents; murder; adultery; stealing; lying; and, coveting. The Ten Commandments expand the summary of the law, and the many stipulations through the rest of Deuteronomy expand upon the Ten Commandments.

As we continue into the detail of the stipulations found in Deuteronomy, each of the ten commands are given expanded specificity and example. The first four commandments are about monotheism—there's only one God. Chapters 6-11 expand on the first command. They encompass the *Shema*, considered to be the most essential prayer in all of Judaism. The commandments in this section progress to a prohibition against idolatrous practices and directions about worship in Chapter 12. Chapter 13 is about honoring the name of God—you shall not take the Lord's name in vain, and chapters 14-16 expand on the fourth command to keep Sabbath. Deuteronomy 16-26 will expand the six commandments governing human relationships.

Ten Commandments
(Deuteronomy 4:44-26:19):

Monotheism (6:1-11:32)

Worship (12:1-32)

Honoring the Name (13:1-14:21)

Sabbath (14:22-16:17)

Honoring Authority (16:18-18:22)

Human Dignity (19:1-22:12)

Sexual Fidelity (22:13-23:18)

Personal Property (23:19-24:22)

Truthfulness (25:1-19)

Contentment (26:1-15)

Succession (31-34)

Limitations of External Law to Sanctify a People

As in the covenant God made with Abraham, there was a major impediment for humans who sought to hold up their end. That impediment was sin, and it created limitations for the covenant between God and Israel. These limitations became obvious almost immediately: right after Moses came down the mountain with the Ten Commandments, he discovered that the high priest, his own brother Aaron, had made an idol, a golden calf, for the people to worship!

When Moses asks his brother why he would do such a thing, Aaron replied that the people, growing impatient with Moses, had "accidentally" dropped their gold into the fire, from which a golden calf emerged. Moses became angry; so angry, in fact, that he smashed the tablets on the ground.

The Greatest Sin

Idolatry was the greatest sin that Israel committed. They committed idolatry *as they were waiting for God's law!* This showed how thoroughly they were trapped in sin; they were so hopeless that it would be funny if it were not so tragic.

Moses punished the people severely for their defiance of God: he ordered them to grind up the idol into a fine dust and *eat* it. The Israelites did so, and then Moses had many of them put to the sword.

Fig. 6. van Rijn, Rembrandt. *Moses Smashing the Tablets of the Law.* 1659. Oil on Canvas. Gemaldegalerie, Berlin. ??

Blessings and Curses

The blessings and curses comprise the fourth section of the covenant. Blessings come to those who follow the stipulations, and curses go to those who break them. This section also describes a ratification ceremony, in which the Israelites stand on two mountains, yelling to each other. They recited the law, then the blessings and curses: "Cursed be anyone who makes an idol or casts an image. Anything abhorrent to the Lord, the work of an artisan, and sets it up in secret. All the people shall respond saying, 'Amen.'" And in saying "Amen," all the people gathered there would say, "So be it to ourselves. That curse is accepted. We've heard the law. We accept the consequences if we break it."

In Deuteronomy 30, Moses said,

"Surely this commandment that I'm giving you today is neither too hard for you nor is it too far away. It's not up in heaven that you should say, 'Who's going to get this commandment for us that we may hear it and observe it?' Neither is it beyond the sea that you should say, 'Who's going to cross the sea to get it for us?' No, this word is very near to you. It's in your mouth. It's in your heart for you to observe. See, I have set before you today life and prosperity, death and adversity. If you obey the commandments of the Lord your God that I am commanding you today by loving the Lord your God, walking in his ways, observing all his commandments, decrees and ordinances, then you shall live, become numerous in the land. The Lord will bless you. And if your heart turns away, you don't hear, are led astray, and bow down to other gods and serve them, then I testify to you today, you will perish. You shall not live long in the land that you are crossing the Jordan to enter and possess. And I call heaven and earth to witness against you today."

Fig. 7. *The Adoration of the Golden Calf.* Before 1634 (oil on canvas) (see 205592-205594 for details), Poussin, Nicolas (1594-1665) National Gallery, London, UK/Bridgeman Images.

Just as there were witnesses in ancient Near Eastern Hittite treaties, the Lord called witnesses, in heaven and earth, to testify. And he reminded the people that they even witnessed against themselves. The people had no alibi, and they had no excuse for breaking the covenant. They must bear full responsibility.

Progressive Nature of Blessings and Curses

The blessings were progressive in nature: greater faithfulness lead to better blessings, while greater unfaithfulness lead to worse curses. The curse may start with crop failure, but ultimately, it could lead to the expulsion from the land of milk and honey. If the people forsook him, God could take away his hedge of protection, letting Israel's enemies come into the land. These enemies could do cruel things to the Israelites, and even bring the Israelites back to their own lands, putting them back into slavery. Thus, they ended up right back where they were before the Exodus: in a foreign country, serving foreign gods and foreign kings.

Blessings and Curses:

Faithfulness leads to progressive blessing, living long in the land

Rebellion leads to progressive curse, leading to exile from the land and death

Issues of Succession

> **Issues of Succession:**
>
> *Fading Memory*
>
> *Leadership Changes and Challenges Caused by Death*
>
> *Biological and Spiritual Transmission of Sin*
>
> *Human Weakness and Doubt*

But what of the succession part? Unlike the Hittite kings, God does not have to worry about his successors, because he does not die. Rather, the issue of succession lay with the divine ambassador, Moses. At the end of Deuteronomy, we see the moment of Moses' testament and death, his final words. Though Moses, the mediator of the covenant, is falling away, the words that God spoke to him and his people do not fall away. The very fact that the covenant is preserved in the form of scripture is what guarantees succession, by ensuring the transmission of the covenant to the people even after the death of Moses.

At the very end of Deuteronomy, Joshua becomes the leader of the Israelites. His story is recounted in the next book of the Bible, the aptly named Book of Joshua. God tells Joshua at the beginning of his leadership: "As I was with Moses, so will I be with you. Be strong and courageous."

God continues by saying that he is the same, yesterday, today, and tomorrow, though earthly leadership changes hands. Even though Moses and other leaders will pass away, God's word will remain the same, and never pass away.

THE TORAH AS THE ENGINE OF THE OLD COVENANT

The Book of Deuteronomy is at the heart of the Old Testament. Everything that has happened before is summarized in Deuteronomy, and everything that comes after it hinges on the teaching and structure of Deuteronomy. Think of Deuteronomy as the engine of the Old Testament. Its fuel—its passion, its fire—is the stories it tells, especially the rescue of the Israelites from Egypt.

Fig. 8. Signorelli, Luca. ***Testament and Death of Moses.*** 1481-1482. Fresco. Sistine Chapel, Vatican.

For why would anyone follow Yahweh? Because their father was a wandering Aramean guided by the LORD. When the Israelites were in cruel bondage in Egypt, the LORD sent a deliverer, Moses. By a mighty hand and an outstretched arm, he destroyed the Egyptians, took them through the Red Sea, and delivered them to the Promised Land. Deuteronomy recounted the story of Abraham, Isaac and Jacob, the story of the Exodus, the creed of Israel; but the thing that drove all of it was the desperate need for humanity to have a savior.

An engine also needs a number of complex parts that work together. All of the working parts in Deuteronomy—the preamble, the prologue, the stipulations, the blessings and curses, and the succession—act together to put into action the fuel of the story.

Constitutional Framework of the Old Testament

Think about the Constitution of the United States. That document, along with the Bill of Rights, provides the governing framework for the United States, and everything else in the U.S. government finds its energy and legitimacy in the Constitution. Judges evaluate our laws according to their constitutionality—in other words, whether they reflect the spirit and letter of the Constitution. Everything is measured against it.

In the same way, as history unfolds for Israel, everything that occurs in the Old Testament is evaluated according to whether it reflects the spirit and letter of Deuteronomy. The instructions about who the Israelites are to be, what they are to do, how they are to do it—all of it is in Deuteronomy.

Interpretative Lens to Evaluate Israel's History

Deuteronomy is also the interpretive lens through which we can look at the history of the Old Covenant and the stories of the kings and their conquests, as well as all of the prophetic books. All of the prophets, including Isaiah, Jeremiah, and minor prophets like Amos and Micah, look back at the events of the Old Testament, and in a sense, they act as God's prosecuting attorneys, defending the constitutional law of Deuteronomy.

They charge that, because the Israelites broke the stipulations of the covenant, they inherited its curses as a result. They grounded themselves in idolatrous worship rather than the love of God. They had not loved each other as neighbors should. God, therefore, chose to withhold his protection. The Israelites should not have been surprised, therefore, that the Assyrians were at their doorstep.

> **Deuteronomy as the Engine of the Old Covenant:**
>
> *Fuel: Deuteronomy is a summary of the Bible from Genesis to Numbers Driver of the rest of the Old Testament*
>
> *Interpretive lens to look at and interpret Israel's history*
>
> *Basis and ground of prophetic lawsuit and promise*
>
> *Manual for reform and reconstruction*

Manual for Reform and Reconstruction

The prophets tended to sound rather judgmental. Their books may be bleak and scary, but they are chosen by God to be the preachers and prosecuting attorneys of the nation of Israel. They know that they must capture the attention of their nation or face certain ruin. Each time that the Israelites realize that they must put things back together and get it right again, they go back to the manual for the ultimate reform and reconstruction—Deuteronomy.

Discovery of the Torah by King Josiah

In 2 Kings 22, the Israelites lose the copy of the Torah in the temple. For several generations, the kings of Israel and Judah (the kingdom of Israel split in two after the death of Solomon. Israel was the "northern" kingdom, Judah the "southern") tried to govern without the guidance of Deuteronomy—a dangerous prospect. Finally, a good king presented in Judah. His name was Josiah, and he was committed to serving God. Hilkiah, the high priest, went into the backroom of the temple, and found the Deuteronomy scroll. Knowing that King Josiah would want to know about the scroll, Hilkiah sent Shaphan, the king's scribe, who brought it to King Josiah. As Shaphan read it to the king, Josiah realized that his people had not been following the covenant of God in a very long time. Josiah instituted national reforms based on the Book of Deuteronomy to bring the nation back into a good relationship with the Lord.

Fig. 9. Bramer, Leonaert. *The Scribe Shaphan Reading the Book of Law to King Josiah.* 1622. Oil on copper. Private collection.]

Theological Implications of the Torah

Deuteronomy is crucial to understanding the rest of the Bible. The grace and redemption that God expresses in Deuteronomy is grounded in the story of the Exodus, while its laws and sanctification show the Israelites how to live out their faith in the life of God.

Just as Exodus is a precursor to Jesus' sacrifice on the cross, so Deuteronomy and the rest of the Torah are a precursor to the Holy Spirit that Jesus' disciples receive along with the New Covenant. But one of the biggest problems of making covenants with human beings is that we tend to forget very quickly what God has asked us to do. All through the Book of Deuteronomy, God tells us not to succumb to forgetfulness from a prideful spirit.

"Beware lest your say in your heart,
'My power and the might of my hand of gotten me this wealth.'
You shall remember the LORD your God,
for it is he who gives you power to get wealth,
that he may confirm his covenant that he swore to your fathers,
as is it this day."
(Deuteronomy 8:17-18)

Remember the word of God. Because it is foreign to our sinful way of life, we are prone to forget it. It is something of which we must continually remind ourselves, every day, and which we must pass on to our children. If we do not constantly seek to remember, then we will not pass it on to our children. Next thing you know, our Bibles will serve as nothing more than coffee table books—a pretty decoration which soon becomes dusty and forgotten. We will no longer know what is in them, and we will not understand them. Like the Israelites of Josiah's day, we will lose the covenant by which God has told us we should live our lives. Remember that this constitution is a gift of God, and that we should cherish it deeply.

Theological Implications:

Grace and Redemption lead to Exodus and the Cross

Law and Sanctification lead to the Torah and the Holy Spirit

CHAPTER 3 NOTES:

CHAPTER 4
Temple: The Kingdom of Priests

Objective: The maturing disciple of Jesus will understand the fundamental role of the tabernacle and the sacrificial system to maintain Israel's relationship with Holy, Holy, Holy God.

INSTRUCTIONS FOR THE TABERNACLE

In the books of Exodus and Leviticus, God gives Moses detailed instructions about the Tabernacle. These instructions can be divided into two broad categories:

- The Tabernacle in Blueprint (Exodus 25-40)
- The Tabernacle in Operation (Leviticus 1-17)

Exodus devotes thirteen of its forty chapters—almost a third—to the tabernacle alone, which shows not only the importance of worship to the community of Israel, but also the importance of Yahweh's physical presence. The wilderness tabernacle fulfilled both of these needs: it brought a sense of order to the worship of God, and it was a tangible reminder of his presence in the midst of his people. Amid the uncertainty and insecurity of the wilderness wanderings, the tabernacle of the Lord would provide a great deal of comfort and security.

HOW TO BUILD THE TABERNACLE:
The Ark of the Covenant and its Cover

The Ark of the Covenant was the most sacred object in the Tabernacle. Physically speaking, it was quite small: approximately 3 ½ feet long, 2 ½ feet wide, and 2 ½ feet high—only slightly larger than a coffee table! However, it was a fearsome thing that contained immense power. When it had to be moved, the people involved were to carry it on poles and never directly touch it, under any circumstance. According to 2 Samuel 6 and 1 Chronicles 13, when a man named Uzzah tried to steady it with his hand, God instantly struck him dead for his disobedience.

The Pentateuch:

Genesis (Preamble)

Exodus (Historic Prologue)

Leviticus (Commandments)

Numbers (Blessings and Curses)

Deuteronomy (Succession)]

How Israel Maintains a Relationship with God:

Tabernacle

Furnishings

Sacrifices

Ordering of Time

tabernacle—(noun)

tab·er·na·cle \ ˈta-bər-na-kəl

a tent sanctuary used by the Israelites during the Exodus

Merriam-Webster Dictionary

At the top of the ark, two golden cherubim shielded the kapporet (cover in Hebrew) with their wings. The kapporet is sometimes called the "mercy seat" or "atonement cover" because of the blood it received on Yom Kippur, the day of atonement. Etymologically, "kapporet" is likely linked to an Egyptian word that is pronounced "kappuriet," which means "the sole of the foot." Thus, the cover of the ark was also God's footstool—the place to meet Yahweh. As God declared in 1 Chronicles 28, Psalms 99 and 132, and Isaiah 60, "I will glorify the place of my feet."

Later, when the new covenant is foretold in Jeremiah 3:16-17, all of Jerusalem becomes the new tabernacle and the footstool of God:

"And when you have multiplied and been fruitful in the land, in those days, declares the LORD, they shall no more say, "The ark of the covenant of the LORD." It shall not come to mind or be remembered or missed; it shall not be made again. 17 At that time Jerusalem shall be called the throne of the LORD, and all nations shall gather to it, to the presence of the LORD in Jerusalem, and they shall no more stubbornly follow their own evil heart." (Jeremiah 3:16-17)

Fig. 1. *Moses and Aaron.* Print. Phillip Medhurst Collection of Bible Illustrations. St. George's Court, Kidderminster, U.K. NEEDS ATTRIBUTION.

Other Furnishings

In addition to the ark, God gave instructions for other objects to be furnished in the Tabernacle. These were: the Table, on which sat holy bread that indicated the presence of God at all times (25:23-30); the Lampstand, which was made of pure gold and followed a pattern shown to Moses on the mountain (25: 31-39); the Altar of Burnt Offering, an outdoor altar made of acacia wood and bronze (27:1-8); the Altar of Incense, on which the High Priest was to burn incense as a fragrant offering to the Lord (30:1-10); and the Bronze Laver, a basin in which the priests would wash with water before their rituals (30:18-21).

The Structure

God also said that the Tabernacle was to follow a specific architecture: there was to be a veil and curtain before the Holy Place (26:31-33), curtains for the Tabernacle (26:1-14), a framework of acacia wood, and a courtyard (27:9-19). All of the furnishings listed above were to go in specific places within the tabernacle, explicitly delineated by God.

Tabernacle Artisans

According to Exodus, the artisans of the Tabernacle were the very first human beings whom God "filled" with the Holy Spirit. Yahweh called these men and vested them with unique wisdom, understanding, knowledge, and ability so that they could accomplish the task of designing and building the Tabernacle and all of its instruments. (31:1-11)

Instructions for Worship

Aaron and his sons Nadab, Abihu, Eleazar, and Ithamar were chosen by God to serve as the priests of his Tabernacle. God provided detailed instructions for these priests; they had to see to the various duties of the Tabernacle, such as Oil for the Lamps, Atonement Money, The Anointing Oil, Recipe for Incense, and Guarding the Sabbath. (27-30) They also had to wear special Priestly Vestments, which included a breast piece of judgment, an ephod (linen robe), a checkered coat, a turban, and a sash (28:4).

With all of these complex and demanding instructions, Yahweh was instilling "covenant faithfulness" in those who worshipped him. He set apart his people to be a unique and holy nation, and warned them to worship as their Holy, Holy, Holy God:

You shall keep the Sabbath, because it is holy for you. Everyone who profanes it shall be put to death."
(Exodus 31:14)

To ensure that all the Israelites knew that he was the one giving them these instructions, Yahweh himself signed and sealed the covenant he gave to Moses:

And he gave to Moses, when he had finished speaking with him on Mount Sinai, the two tablets of the testimony, tablets of stone, written with the finger of God.
(Exodus 31:18)

Detailed Instructions are Given for:

Holy Place Veil and Curtain

Tabernacle Curtains

Framework

Courtyard

Tabernacle Furniture:

Holy of Holies
(Ark of the Covenant)

Sanctuary
(Candlestick, Altar of Incense, Showbread Table)

Courtyard
(Altar of Sacrifice, Water Basin)

Other Furniture in the Tabernacle:

Table

Lampstand

Altar of Burnt Offering

Altar of Incense

Bronze Laver

Structure

Specific instructions for Priestly Vestments:

Ephod

Breast Pieces

Other Vestments

COVENANT BROKEN:
Golden Calf Story Literary Structure

Chiastic Structure of the Covenant Broken in Exodus:

   A People act and Aaron reacts (32:1-6)
      B Yahweh's two utterances: Yahweh spoke, Yahweh said (32:7-10)
         C Moses intercedes (32:11-14)
            D Moses goes down the mountain (32:15-20)
               E Judgment: Investigative phase (32:21-25)
                  F Opportunity for repentance (32:26a)
               E' Judgment: Executive phase (32:26b-29)
            D' Moses goes up the mountain (32:30)
         C' Moses intercedes (32:31-32)
      B' Yahweh's two utterances: Yahweh said, Yahweh spoke (32:33-33:3)
   A' Yahweh acts, and people react (33:4-6)]

Box with Chiastic Structure of the Tabernacle in Exodus:

   A Tabernacle planned (24:12-27:21)
      B Priestly instructions (28-30)
         C Craftsmen's directions (31:1-11)
            D Sabbath instructions (31:12-18)
               E Covenant broken (32)
                  E' Covenant renewed (33-34)
            D' Sabbath reminder (35:1-3)
        C' Craftsmen and construction (35:4-38:31)
      B' Priests prepared (39)
   A' Tabernacle completed (40:1-33)]

Impatience

According to Exodus, the Golden-Calf idol was a result of the Israelites' impatience; they felt that "Moses delayed to come down from the mountain" (32:1) This is a recurring theme: the people were impatient even when God gave them manna. They were again impatient when he gave them quail. They were yet again impatient when he gave them water. And now they were impatient as God was giving them the law!

When Moses asked Aaron why he would encourage such blatant

idolatry, he replied:

"Let not the anger of my lord burn hot. You know the people, that they are set on evil. For they said to me, 'Make us gods who shall go before us. As for this Moses, the man who brought us up out of the land of Egypt, we do not know what has become of him.'
So I said to them, 'Let any who have gold take it off.'
So they gave it to me,
and I threw it into the fire, and out came this calf."
(Exodus 32:22)

To hide his own responsibility, Aaron painted himself as a passive victim of the people's whims rather than the ringleader who in 32:2-6 was the one who personally asked the people to take off their gold, fashioned the gold into a calf with a "graving tool," built an altar, and made a proclamation to feast!

chiasmus—(noun)
chi·as·mus \ kī-ˈaz-məs, kē-
an inverted relationship between the syntactic elements of parallel phrases
Merriam-Webster Dictionary

The Intercession of Moses

Yahweh responded to the golden calf with indignation and declared to Moses his desire to entirely "consume" the Israelites in judgment with Moses alone left to reconstitute a faithful nation.

Just as Abraham had pleaded for God to show mercy to the people of Sodom and Gomorrah, Moses appealed to Yahweh's reputation in the world and the covenant he had made with Abraham about his descendants. Moses understood the heart of Yahweh: more than anything, God wants to be gloriously known by the peoples of the world, and he always keeps his covenant promises.

After Moses interceded, Yahweh decided to relent. What does this episode teach us about praying and interceding for others?

"But now if you will forgive their sin—but if not, please blot me out of your book that you have written."
(Exodus 32:32)

Indictment and Judgment

Though the Lord relented from "the disaster he had spoken of bringing on his people", he still imposed a grave sentence for their disobedience. Moses faithfully represented the wrath of God by breaking the two stone tablets of the Covenant.

He then crushed the calf into a fine powder and made the people drink that powder. He interrogated Aaron and gave the Israelites an opportunity to return to the Lord:

"Who is on the Lord's side? Come to me."
(Exodus 32:26)

Those who came were the "sons of Levi". They became the executors of God's judgment upon their "brothers, companions and neighbors," 3,000 of whom fell that day at the swords of the sons of Levi.

After this was done, Moses again made intercession for the people, offering God his own life in exchange for the lives of his people. But God declared that his judgment would be complete only after the day of his visitation:

"Nevertheless, in the day when I visit, I will visit their sin upon them. Then the LORD sent a plague on the people, because they made the calf, the one that Aaron made."
(Exodus 32:34-35)

Repentance and Mercy

The Lord commanded Moses to lead the people to the Promised Land without him. Throughout the story, the answer to the question, "To whom does the nation of Israel belong?" is kept in doubt. For a time, it seemed that Yahweh was prepared to simply hand them off to Moses!

The Israelites do attempt to make amends to God. In "stripping themselves" of their ornaments, as the Lord told them to do, they began the process of reconciliation with him. In truth, however, the most important factor in this reconciliation was the special relationship that Yahweh had with Moses. He treated Moses as a confidant, and at the "tent of meeting," Yahweh would even speak to Moses "face to face as a man speaks to his friend." (33:11) Because he trusted Moses, he knew that the people, though prone to wander, would find their way in the desert.

To behold the Lord is an awesome privilege that he gave to no one else in Exodus; but Paul says that we, saved by Christ, receive this privilege through the Holy Spirit:

Yes, to this day whenever Moses is read a veil lies over their hearts. But when one turns to the Lord, the veil is removed. Now the Lord

is the Spirit, and where the Spirit of the Lord is, there is freedom. And we all, with unveiled face, beholding the glory of the Lord, are being transformed into the same image from one degree of glory to another.
For this comes from the Lord who is the Spirit.
(2 Corinthians 3:15-18)

The Presence and the Face

After the golden calf, it was by no means clear that Yahweh would continue to lead his people and dwell in their midst. But Moses did not give up his faith in the Lord that had led him thus far. He was persistent in preserving his nation's relationship with Yahweh:

Now therefore, if I have found favor in your sight, please show me now your ways, that I may know you in order to find favor in your sight. Consider too that this nation is your people."
(Exodus 33:13)

God rewards Moses' faith and humility with a glorious moment. Yahweh would reveal his glory to him, not in its fullness, but in its "goodness". (33:19) Glory, in its goodness, is the visible manifestation of the nature and attributes of God. As Yahweh passed before Moses, he revealed his nature and attributes:

The LORD descended in the cloud and stood with him there, and proclaimed the name of the LORD. The LORD passed before him and proclaimed, "The LORD, the LORD, a God merciful and gracious, slow to anger, and abounding in steadfast love and faithfulness, keeping steadfast love for thousands, forgiving iniquity and transgression and sin, but who will by no means clear the guilty, visiting the iniquity of the fathers on the children and the children's children, to the third and the fourth generation."
(Exodus 34:5-7)

God renewed his covenant with Israel by giving a new set of Tablets inscribed with the Ten Words. Moses made the tablets, and Yahweh himself inscribed the Words. (34:28)

From then on, whenever Moses would come out from the Tent of Meeting, his face would shine with the reflected Glory of the Lord. It was so bright that a veil had to be placed over it whenever he spoke

---

Box with Ten Commandments:

Love and Worship God
(Commandments 1-4)

Love and Respect Humans, Made in God's Image
(Commandments 5-10)

Box with Three Types of Law:

Moral Laws

Civil Laws

Religious Laws

the word of the Lord, because the glory inspired a great fear of the Lord in the people. (34:29-35)

And the Word became flesh and dwelt among us, and we have seen his glory, glory as of the only Son from the Father, full of grace and truth.
(John 1:14)

The Offering of the Tabernacle

The tabernacle construction was truly a labor of love for the Lord—a "freewill offering." The people contributed all of the gold, jewels and other materials, much as they had done for the golden calf; but this time, they did so not because of their selfishness, but because their "hearts stirred them" and the "spirit moved them;" they had a "willing heart." The offering was so bounteous that the craftsmen did not know what to do with all the materials that were brought to them. The people even had to be "restrained from bringing" (36:6) any more material, "for they had what was sufficient to do the work, and more." (36:7)

Fig. 7. Slide 11. NEEDS ATTRIBUTION.

The Glory of the Lord

The book of Exodus ends on a glorious note: after the offering is complete, and all of Yahweh's instructions for building and assembly of the Tabernacle are fulfilled, "Moses finished the work." (40:33) Israel was now on the march toward the Promised Land, and the Presence and Glory of the Lord that had once seemed so close to abandoning them was now leading them and dwelling in their midst. They had learned that man does not live on bread alone, but on every word that comes from the mouth of the Lord. They had learned to trust his Word of the Lord as it was given through Moses, and they had learned to be humble and wait patiently on the Lord.

Then the cloud covered the tent of meeting, and the glory of the LORD filled the tabernacle. And Moses was not able to enter the tent of meeting because the cloud settled on it, and the glory of the LORD filled the tabernacle. Throughout all their journeys, whenever the cloud was taken up from over the tabernacle, the people of Israel would set out. But if the cloud was not taken up,

then they did not set out till the day that it was taken up. For the cloud of the LORD was on the tabernacle by day, and fire was in it by night, in the sight of all the house of Israel throughout all their journeys.
(Exodus 40:34-38)

Structure of Leviticus

Part 1: The Laws of Acceptable Approach to God: Sacrifice (1-17)
    The Laws of Acceptable Approach to God (1-7)
    The Laws of the Priests (8-10)
    The Laws of Israel regarding Purity (11-15)
    The Laws of National Atonement (16-17)

Part 2: The Laws of Acceptable Walk with God: Sanctification (18-27)
    The Laws of Sanctification for the People (18-20)
    The Laws of Sanctification for the Priesthood (21-22)
    The Laws of Sanctification in Worship (23-24)
    The Laws of Sanctification in the Land of Canaan (25-26)
    The Laws of Sanctification Through Vows (27)

For there is no distinction: for all have sinned and fall short of the glory of God, and are justified by his grace as a gift, through the redemption that is in Christ Jesus, whom God put forward as a propitiation by his blood, to be received by faith.
(Romans 3:22-25)

PART 1
The Laws of Acceptable Approach to God: Sacrifice (1-17)

The first seventeen chapters of Leviticus describe the laws which govern how Israel is to be a Holy Nation and how they are to worship God in the Tabernacle. Through these laws, Israel was to become a people completely sacrificed and acceptable to God.

The Laws of Acceptable Approach to God (1-7)

The Israelites were to make five different kinds of sacrifices to God, for different purposes: burnt offerings (1:3-17), grain offerings (2:1-16), peace offerings (3:1-17), sin offerings (4:1-35), and guilt offerings (5:1-6:7). The first three kinds of offerings were regularly made

Five Types of Sacrifices:
Burnt offering (1:3-17)
Grain offering (2:1-16)
Peace offering (3:1-17)
Sin offering (4:1-35)
Guilt offering (5:1-6:7)

by those who were in fellowship and right relationship with God, while the last two were made by those who were out of fellowship with God because of their sin.

How to Approach God When in Fellowship
Burnt Offering (1:3-17)

When a burnt offering was made, it would follow a specific pattern: the offeror would bring a bull without defect to the tent of meeting (1:3). There were also the options to offer a male sheep or goat (1:10-13), or birds, specifically turtledoves or pigeons, to the altar as burnt offerings (1:14-17). The offeror would lean his hand on the bull and kill it (1:4-5). Next, the sons of Aaron, or priests, would throw the bull's blood against the altar, flay its skin, cut it into pieces, wash its entrails and legs with water, and burn it all for the Lord to enjoy (1:5-9).

> **Burnt Offering Steps:**
> *Bringing the offering (Offeror)*
> *Hand-leaning (Offeror)*
> *Slaughtering the animal*
> *Splashing the blood (Sons of Aaron)*
> *Flaying the skin (Sons of Aaron)*
> *Dissecting the animal (Sons of Aaron)*
> *Washing*
> *Burning (Sons of Aaron)*

The burnt offering was a very costly sacrifice, because an animal without defect was of great value in that time. Its death represented the offeror's life, which was completely handed over to Yahweh. No one could offer this sacrifice properly unless he was prepared to follow God wholeheartedly, just as Noah (Gen 6:9; 8:20) and Abraham did (17:1; 15:6). In Psalm 51:17-19, King David tells us that a broken spirit and a broken and contrite heart leads to an acceptable burnt offering to the Lord.

The burnt offering was given to propitiate (or satisfy) the wrath of God against the sinful condition of the human heart. God required that sacrifices be made for the sins of the Israelites, and the parallel between the sacrifice of a burnt offering for the sins of an individual and the sacrifice of Jesus for the sins of the whole world would have been very meaningful to the earliest Christians. It is why, in the Book of Common Prayer, we refer to Jesus Christ as the only "full, perfect, and sufficient, oblation and satisfaction for the sins of the whole world."

Grain (or Loyalty) Offering (2:1-16)

The purpose of a grain offering to the Lord was to remind him of the covenantal relationship that existed between him and the offeror, and of the loyalty that the offeror had to God. There is a subtle but crucial distinction to be made between the burnt and grain offerings: whereas it was the *person* (*adam* in Hebrew) who offered a burnt offering, it was the *soul* (*nepes* in Hebrew) that would offer the grain offering. It was the offering of one's soul as a pleasant, though not physical, aroma to the Lord. Human souls are by nature insular and self-centered. In making the offering, a person would demonstrate to the Lord that they were, and wished to remain, Yahweh-centered.

Peace (or Fellowship) Offering (3:1-17)

The peace offering reflected an intimate communion with the Lord. The offeror, as in the burnt offering, leaned his hand on the offering, symbolically identifying the animal with him. The animal thus gave his life for the offeror. The egocentric and complacent portions (i.e. the fat) of the heart were consumed on the altar as an acceptable sacrifice.

This offering was made at times of thanksgiving and when one wished to make a vow of dedication to the Lord. Fellowship with the Lord could only come when a person destroyed their egocentric nature.

How to approach God When Out of Fellowship
Sin Offerings and Guilt offerings (4:1-35, 5:1-6:7)

The sin offerings and guilt offerings were for unintentional and intentional sins, respectively. Both kinds of sin carried a cost to the sinner and would put a person, priest or even an entire congregation out of fellowship with the Lord. Appropriate sacrifices had to be made to restore the relationship with God.

Keep a close watch on yourself and on the teaching. Persist in this, for by so doing you will save both yourself and your hearers.
(1 Timothy 4:16)

The Laws of the Priests (8-10)
The consecration of the priesthood (8:1-9:24)

The ordination of Aaron and his sons demonstrated that sin was a universal phenomenon. Even those who received the holiest of callings, ministering in the tabernacle of the Lord, were sinners in desperate need of forgiveness and atonement.

However, Leviticus makes an important contrast between Moses and

Aaron: Moses offered sacrifices for Aaron and his sons, but not for himself. Aaron angered the Lord by leading the people into idolatry, but God was pleased with Moses and his leadership, and so Moses did not need to make a sacrifice (though he would deeply anger the Lord in Numbers 20 by not trusting him).

Moses in this passage embodies personal holiness, which is one's ability to dwell in the presence of God. For each Israelite, the barriers to personal holiness were sin, uncleanness and self-centeredness. Holiness was above all a matter of the heart, and it required mediation through costly personal and communal sacrifice.

> **propitiation**—(noun)
> pro·pi·ti·a·tion \
> prō-pi-shē-ˈā-shən
> an atoning sacrifice
> *Merriam-Webster Dictionary*

Failure of the priesthood (10:1-2)

Two of Aaron's sons, Nadab and Abihu, failed to take the holiness of God seriously. With their unauthorized fire, they demonstrated their disregard for the Holy, and God burned them to death as a result.

The calling to be a priest in the temple was not a light one. Priests were to carry out their duties with exacting precision, in accord with the command of the Lord. Sin was an incredibly serious matter for God and for the Israelites. The Mediators of God's covenant could not deviate from God's message or actions as they led the people of God into a relationship with God. If they did, they would be leading them away from God—which, as we will see, happened all too often later in the Old Testament.

Clean and Unclean

The words "sin" and "unclean" are not synonyms, but they are clearly related. One could become unclean or defiled from breaking one of God's commands, such as the ones pertaining to sexual morality (Lev. 18). But one could also become unclean for other reasons, such as obtaining leprosy (a horrific skin disease), touching blood or a dead body, eating unclean foods, or menstruating (Lev. 11-15).

Whatever is clean (*tahor* in Hebrew) becomes defiled by contact with whatever is unclean [tamei in Hebrew]. Uncleanness overcomes the holy and the clean. The prophet Haggai asked the priests of Israel:

"If someone carries holy meat in the fold of his garment and touches with his fold bread or stew or wine or oil or any kind of food, does it become holy?" The priests answered and said, "No." Then Haggai said, "If someone who is unclean by contact with a dead body touches any of these, does it become unclean?" The priests answered and said, "It does become unclean."

Then Haggai answered and said, "So is it with this people, and with this nation before me, declares the LORD, and so with every work of their hands.
And what they offer there is unclean."
(Haggai 2:12-14)

Clean and unclean is concerned with the external condition. Dirty things make clean things dirty—not the other way around. Ceremonially and ritual cleanliness set apart the people of Israel as the appropriate condition for fellowship with God.

By contrast, sin is an internal condition of the heart. Sinful actions become matters of legal justice; sin demands a just, legal verdict. Sinful acts provoke a verdict of condemnation because sins are crimes against God and neighbor. Because there is no cure for our incorrigible sinful nature, the judgment for our sins is the penalty of death.

These issues are a point of major discussion in the Gospels and the Letters of Paul as the new promises of God in Jesus are expanded to include the Gentiles. With the new covenant, Jesus sets aside issues of clean and unclean and focuses on internal root issues of the sinful heart:

There is nothing outside a person that by going into him can defile him, but the things that come out of a person are what defile him.... For from within, out of the heart of man, come evil thoughts, sexual immorality, theft, murder, adultery, coveting, wickedness, deceit, sensuality, envy, slander, pride, foolishness. All these evil things come from within, and they defile a person."
(Mark 7:15, 21-22)

Self-Hiding and Self-Uncovering before the Lord

Both sin and uncleanness lead to a self-hiding from the Lord: sin because of guilt, and uncleanness because of impurity or dirtiness. Uncleanliness and sin lead to shame. Shame comes rather naturally to humans: when Adam and Eve became aware of their nakedness, they sewed fig leaves and "hid themselves from the presence of Yahweh among the trees." (Gen. 3:7-8) For how could they approach a holy, holy, holy God? How could they enter his presence without their every fault, blemish and defilement being exposed? They come to believe (absurdly, of course) that their best option is to hide from God—and we are often inclined to do the same.

Rather, God wanted the Israelites to uncover themselves and their sin before him. Sacrifices made it possible for the Lord's holiness and just wrath to be satisfied (or propitiated) and for a sinful and shameful people to dwell in the presence of Yahweh. Sin required a penalty to be paid, and uncleanness required washing and healing. In both cases, the uncovering of self before the Lord's presence left the worshiper holy, clean, and free.

In their relationships with one another and with their surrounding natures and cultures, the Israelites had countless occasions both to sin and to become unclean. God's aim and calling to the Israelites was for them to "be holy as I am holy". While the laws of the first half of Leviticus detail how to approach and dwell in the presence of a holy God, the Laws of the second half of Leviticus explain how Israel was to walk in that holiness of life in the contexts of their relationships with God, one another and the surrounding pagan cultures of Egypt, and the land of Canaan.

"And this shall be a statute forever for you, that an atonement may be made for the people of Israel once in the year because of all their sins."
(Leviticus 16:34)

The Day of Atonement (Leviticus 16-17)

The central command and "hinge" of the book of Leviticus is chapter 17, which describes The Day of Atonement (*Yom Kippur* in Hebrew). This annual ritual was the single most important one for the Israelites: it included atonement for the Holy of Holies, the priests, and all the people, and ended with the expulsion of the "Azazel" goat (or scapegoat) from the camp, which reflected the spiritual expulsion of sin.

The Day of Atonement was different from all the other sacrifices in the physical orientation and direction of its ritual sacrifices. On the Day of Atonement, rituals happen outside rather than inside and the other sacrifices happen inside rather than outside. The Day of Atonement is the sacrifice of the entire sanctuary, and it makes all other sacrifices acceptable and possible. In the same way, the sacrifice of Jesus on the cross as a sacrifice of atonement (Romans 3:21) makes our sacrifice of ourselves as living sacrifices (Romans 12:1) acceptable and pleasing to God.

The Goat for Yahweh and the Goat for Azazel

"And Aaron shall cast lots over the two goats, one lot for the Lord and the other lot for Azazel." (Leviticus 16:8) Traditionally, Azazel has been translated as "scapegoat" (ez meaning "goat" and azel meaning "going away"). However, it may also be a fallen angel, or a demonic presence (1906 Jewish Encyclopedia). If this is the case, then to send the goat into "the wilderness to Azazel" (16:10) was to send the sins of the people back to their source, Satan.

The practices of the Israelites were in sharp contrast to the practices of the Egyptians and Canaanites. The abominations and unclean acts expressly forbidden in Leviticus are incorporated into the practices of the surrounding cultures. Israel is in a covenantal relationship with Yahweh; they are not to serve foreign gods and "walk in their statutes". Hence, "You shall follow my rules and keep my statutes and walk in them. I am Yahweh *your God."* (18:4)

The calling of Israel was to be a Holy Nation. "You shall be holy, for I, Yahweh your God am holy. (19:2) All the people of Israel were specifically called to *holiness of life*. Holiness of life takes place within the many different kinds of relationships, such as sex, marriage, family, work, and interaction with foreigners and strangers. The people were to engage only in those relationships that God intended for them to have, and only in the ways that he intended. Those who kept the commandments would have life, but those who disobeyed the Lord's rules and statutes "shall surely die," just as God had warned Adam and Eve in the garden. (Genesis 2:17)

Laws of Sexual Sins (18)

The Israelites were to distinguish themselves from their unclean neighbors by staying faithful to the distinctiveness of marriage, with male and female as complements to one another. As Genesis 2 points out, animals were clearly not suitable helpmates for Adam or any man. In addition, men were called to leave behind the households of their mothers and fathers to find their wives. Thus, acts of homosexuality, bestiality and incest were all forbidden for the Israelites, as they were all contrary to the holiness of life to which God had called them.

The Lord's aim for the Israelites was that they would be fruitful and multiply. If they protected the sanctity of marriage, they would be blessed with fertility and an abundance of descendants.

Sin:

As a condition, sin leads to shame, which leads to isolation and separation

As an action, sin leads to guilt, which leads to condemnation and judgment

> **glean**—(verb) \'glēn
> to gather grain or other produce left by reapers
> *Merriam-Webster Dictionary*

> **Ordering of Times and Seasons:**
>
> *Weekly Sabbath:* on the seventh day with no work
>
> *Annual Festival Days:* Passover, Unleavened Bread, First Fruits, Weeks, Trumpets, Day of Atonement, Booths
>
> *Sabbath Year:* on the seventh year with the land resting
>
> *Jubilee Year:* on the 15th year with debts forgiven and slaves freed

> **Festival Days by Season:**
>
> *Spring:* Passover, Unleavened Bread, First Fruits
>
> *Summer:* Pentecost
>
> *Fall:* Trumpets, Atonement, Tabernacles

Laws of social order (19)

Many of the laws in this chapter protected the dignity of the individual person who was made in the royal image of God, both male and female, rich and poor, young and old, slave and free, neighbor and stranger, citizen and alien.

If the Israelites kept all the laws of social order, their relationships with one another would be characterized by honor, love and life. The fabric of their community would be strong and united. The rich would care for the poor by leaving the gleaning on the edge for their provision. It is only when these basic values and commands to love one another are not upheld that society begins to disintegrate.

Laws of Distinctiveness

There are multiple intriguing laws interspersed within these general themes. Some of these laws, such as those that encourage the separation of crops and livestock and prohibit the mixing of fabrics (19:19), may seem arbitrary to modern ears. But the prohibitions against mixing of seeds and livestock sought to preserve the distinctiveness of the things which God made. To mix different forms of life in this way was, in a sense, to tamper with life itself.

Israel also was to be distinct in their appearance and dress from the surrounding cultures. The commands on hair and beards and fabrics may have existed in part to create this external distinctiveness. It may also have set apart the people's common garments from the Holy of Holies and the high priest's garments—which were, as you might recall, made from mixed fabrics.

Seven Feasts (23)

Leviticus mandates a weekly Sabbath to the Lord and seven solemn feast days to mark the history of Israel's relationship with God and their ongoing relationship of blessing with Yahweh. In the spring, there were to be the feasts of Passover, Unleavened Bread, and First Fruits; in the summer, there was the feast of Pentecost; and in the fall, there were the feasts of Trumpets, Atonement, and Tabernacles.

These annual celebrations and sacrifices would serve, above all, to retain the memory of God's mighty acts on behalf of Israel and their need for ongoing redemption, provision and relationship.

"For it is to me that the people of Israel are servants. They are my servants whom I brought out of the Land of Egypt. I am the LORD your God."

(Leviticus 25:55)

Jubilee (25)

Every fiftieth year was to be a Jubilee year. The number seven and its multiples are formative for Israel, as God was making a *new creation* in the people. The weekly Sabbath, the Sabbath Year (every seventh year), and the Sabbath of Sabbaths (every seven weeks of years, or every forty-ninth year) all marked Israel as the new creation of God. There was a recognition that, over time, all relationships would get out of balance despite people's best efforts. The Jubilee year thus provided a regular reset and a fresh start for society, in which property rights were returned, burdensome debts were forgiven, and slaves were released. In order for Jubilee to truly work, the people had to recognize that the land and the people ultimately belonged to the LORD.

Blessings and Curses

The laws of God are "your life," Moses told the people. It was in keeping *all* of the Laws of God that a new Garden of Eden could be established, where the kingdom of God was on earth as in heaven. Yahweh promised increasing blessing for covenant faithfulness and holiness. However, he also promised grave consequences for violating the laws of God. Both the Blessings and the Curses grew in magnitude, depending on the strength of the people's commitment to Yahweh, or their failure to turn away from sin and walk in holiness.

"But if they confess their iniquity and the iniquity of their fathers in their treachery that they committed against me, and also in walking contrary to me, so that I walked contrary to them and brought them into the land of their enemies—if then their uncircumcised heart is humbled and they make amends for their iniquity, then I will remember my covenant with Jacob, and I will remember my covenant with Isaac and my covenant with Abraham, and I will remember the land.

(Leviticus 26:40-42)

The Presence of Yahweh:

Walked with **Adam** *In the cool of the day*

Moses *met with God in the meeting tent*

David *was given instructions for a permanent temple*

Solomon *built the temple*

The **temple was destroyed** *by the Babylonians in 586 BC*

The **temple was rebuilt** *by Ezra and Nehemiah after the Cyrus Edict*

The **temple was renovated** *by Herod the Great*

The **temple was destroyed** *by the Romans in 70 AD*

Problems and Weaknesses:

God doesn't dwell in structures made with human hands

The blood of animals could never take away sin

The sin, weakness and finiteness of the Levite priesthood

The sacrifice that God desires is a broken and contrite heart

CHAPTER 4 NOTES:

CHAPTER 5
Promised Land: Entering into Sabbath Rest

Objective: The maturing disciple of Jesus will understand the fundamental role of the Promised Land as God's gift of Sabbath blessing to the nation of Israel.

GOD'S COVENANTS OF THE OLD TESTAMENT

As we have learned, God makes five major covenants in the Old Testament, with Adam, Noah, Abraham, Moses, and David respectively. In the New Testament, he makes a sixth covenant with Jesus. To understand Scripture, one must know all of these covenants, what they meant for these men (and what they mean for us), and how they inform each other. In this chapter, we will focus on the significance of the Promised Land in the covenants.

The Abrahamic Covenant

God made seven promises in the Abrahamic covenant, in the form of "I will" statements: "And I will make you a great nation, and I will bless you and make your name great, so that you will be a blessing." (Genesis 12:2) "I will bless those who bless you and him who dishonors you I will curse, and in you all the families of the earth shall be blessed." (Genesis 12:3) And, "To you and your offspring I will give this land." (Genesis 12:7)

That land would, of course, become the nation of Israel—known also as the land of Canaan, the Promised Land, Israel and Palestine.

Renewal of the Abrahamic Covenant

The covenant with Abraham did not end with him: in Genesis 12, God renewed his promises with Abraham's son Isaac and his grandson Jacob. Together, they made up the three biblical patriarchs upon whom the Israelite society was founded.

Seven "I Will" Promises:

I will make you a great nation

I will give you a great name

I will bless you

I will bless those who bless you

I will curse those who curse you

I will bless all nations of the world through you

I will give you this land

With Jacob, God also spelled out the covenant more explicitly than he had with Abraham. One night, Jacob wrestled with an angel sent by God, who hit him in his hip and gave him a permanent limp. But Jacob had fought all night and survived, and the angel gave him a new name, Israel, which means "one who wrestles with God." Jacob would go on to have 12 sons, who together would form the 12 tribes of Israel. Like Jacob, the nation of Israel would continually wrestle with the Lord and resist his will for them—and yet it would always survive, by his grace.

Signs of God's Promises

Abraham has been called the father of faith because he truly trusted in the Lord, even when God tested him by ordering him to sacrifice his son Isaac. In the New Testament, the epistle to the Hebrews holds Abraham up as a prime example of faith (Hebrews 11:8-12). But even he doubted that God would indeed deliver on his promise to give him the land. The Lord answered this doubt by putting a sign in Abraham's flesh. This sign showed that God would make him a great nation and make a promise to his descendants: "I will surely multiply your offspring as the stars of heaven and as the sand that is on the seashore" (Genesis 22:17).

That sign was circumcision—a covenant with Abraham's seed in a quite literal sense, and a physical reminder than that God's promises were for Abraham, his children and his children's children. Circumcision set Abraham apart from all other men of his time, and it would later set God's chosen people apart from the uncircumcised Gentiles who surrounded them.

God also showed that he would keep his promise with his instruction by passing between the halves of animal carcasses. This showed that God would take on all of the responsibility and risk (such as it was) of giving Abraham and his descendants the land.

It was a one-sided covenant. God recognized that human beings would not keep their promises—not even Abraham. Nevertheless, his promises are certain and sure, and eternal in nature.

The covenant continued to Abraham's descendants, the Israelites:

"And they shall come back here in the fourth generation, for the iniquity of the Amorites is not yet complete."
(Genesis 15:16)

Although there were other people—the Amorites—already living in the Promised Land at that time, the land did not belong to them. But it was not God's plan for Abraham to fight and remove them himself. Instead, God declared that their removal would take place much later: it would wait until the fourth generation, when the Amorites' sin became so great that they invited judgment upon themselves.

Thus, the return of the Israelites to the Promised Land was a gift and a grace for them, and a sign of judgment for the Amorites.

THE PENTATEUCH: The Books of Moses

The Mosaic covenant appears in the first five books of the Bible—Genesis, Exodus, Leviticus, Numbers and Deuteronomy. Collectively, these five books are known as the Pentateuch, the Torah, or the books of Moses.

Tradition holds that Moses wrote the first five books of the Bible. However, these books saw some revision over time. For example, the names of certain key locations changed over the years, and a scribe might, as a courtesy to the reader, identify a certain Egyptian city as *Ramesses*, its contemporaneous name, rather than *Avaris*, as it would have been known in Moses' time.

In addition, the end of Deuteronomy describes Moses' death, and it is unlikely that Moses wrote it himself. Clearly, some editorial work went into shaping the Torah into its final form. The books of the Torah are, however, written in the voice of Moses, and most traditional scholars say that Moses is the primary author.

The Book of Joshua

Joshua is the sixth book in the Bible and the first book following the Torah. Given that the book's namesake Joshua is the central figure of the story, a few biblical scholars believe that Joshua himself is the author; however, because of the lack of evidence, most scholars consider the author unknown.

The Book of Joshua marks a new beginning for the people of Israel and a major turning point in their history. The seventh "I will" of God's covenant with Abraham was implemented as the Israelites entered the Promised Land. Because Moses did not fully trust in the Lord, Yahweh had forbidden him from entering the Promised Land (Deuteronomy 3:25-27). Instead, he gave the honor and duty of settling the land to Joshua, Moses' deputy, who took charge of the Israelites upon Moses' death. It is only after Joshua becomes leader that the people enter Canaan.

The change of leadership, therefore, was also a change of course for the Israelites. The days with Moses of receiving the covenant and wandering in the wilderness were over; now, with Joshua, it was time to take the land that God had promised to Abraham.

The book of Joshua is divided into four parts. In the first part, the Israelites cross the threshold into the Promised Land; in the second part, they take the land from the people already living there; in the third part, they divide that land into 12 regions, for each of the 12 tribes; finally, in the fourth part, they work to keep the land by serving God.

The Book of Joshua:

Cross: *Entry into Canaan (Joshua 1-5)*

Take: *The Battle for Canaan (Joshua 6-12)*

Divide: *Allocating Canaan (Joshua 13-21)*

Serve: *Keeping Canaan (Joshua 22-24)*

Yahweh Renews His Covenant Promise

"Just as I was with Moses, so will I be with you.
I will not leave you or forsake you."
(Joshua 1:5)

God told Joshua to be strong and courageous, and to remember that he would be with him through it all. With Yahweh's blessing, the Israelites would inherit the Promised Land.

"Only be strong and very courageous,
being careful to do according to all the law
that Moses my servant commanded you.
Do not turn from it to the right hand or to the left,
that you may have good success wherever you go.
This Book of the Law shall not depart from your mouth,
but you shall meditate on it day and night,
so that you may be careful to do according to all that is
written in it. For then you will make your way prosperous,
and then you will have good success.
Have I not commanded you?"
(Joshua 1:7-9)

Fig. 1. Church, Frederic Edwin (American, 1826-1900). *Moses Viewing the Promised Land.* 1846. Oil on Caradboard. Private Collection.

God reminded Joshua not to deviate from the law—to follow God's straight and narrow path, straying neither to the left nor the right. If Joshua would obey the Lord faithfully, then he and his people would be blessed. Implicit, of course, was a warning that any disobedience could lead to severe consequences. Because the law was the historic recounting of God's redemption through the Exodus, trusting in it meant trusting that God would, in fact, bring redemption to his people. It meant taking a step out in faith, with strength and courage, believing that the Lord would see his people through, even against the mighty enemies they faced and feared. And it applied to Joshua's generation and future generations, just as it had for Moses'.

Preparation for Victory

To understand what happens next, it is necessary to return briefly to the Book of Numbers. Numbers recounts the journey through the wilderness. Moses, Aaron and the Israelites arrived at the edge of the Promised Land rather quickly. It did not take them anywhere near 40 years to go from Egypt to Canaan! The delay in reaching the Promised Land, rather, was in waiting for God's command to enter, which did not come in the time of Moses. Thus, the Israelites waited at the border for many years, in the Wilderness of Zin.

In the meantime, they decided to send spies into the Negeb in order to prepare. The spies observed many different cities during their operation. The spies saw many wonderful fruits in the Valley of Eschol: grapes, pomegranates, and figs. These fruits were a sign that the land was as bountiful as God had promised; it was truly a "land flowing with milk and honey." (Exodus 33:3) Their trust in the Lord had proved to be well-founded.

Fig. 2. Lanfranco, Giovanni. *The Messengers Return from Canaan.* 1621-24. Oil on canvas. J. Paul Getty Museum, Los Angeles.

But the spies saw other things as well: when they went to Hebron, they saw the Nephilim, descendants of Anak. The Nephilim, or Anakites were giants, and the spies reported that they felt as small as "grasshoppers" in comparison! (Numbers 13:33) Defeating such a powerful people would require a lot of strength, courage—and faith.

And they were not the only people living there. There were Hittites, Jebusites, Amorites, Canaanites, and other tribes as well. Though one of the spies, Caleb, wanted to fight them all at once, the others said that they were not prepared or strong enough to do so. Instead, they went back to report what they had found to the Israelites.

When the people heard the spies' report, they were afraid. Many of them wanted to go back to Egypt. Even Moses and Aaron fell on their faces and did not challenge them, for they saw what seemed like an impossible task before them.

Only Joshua and Caleb wanted to enter the land and fight for it. Rather than believing in the long odds that conventional wisdom would give to the Israelites, they believed and trusted in the promise that the Lord had made to Abraham, and did not fear the other tribes or nations. If God could rout the mighty Egyptians, and cast the pharaoh's fearsome chariots into the sea, why should they doubt that he could give them the Promised Land?

But the rest continued to have the slave mentality instilled in them by the Egyptians. They were governed by a fear of men, which, incredibly, exceeded their fear of God. In that moment, they did not trust in God, and they shrunk back from entering the Promised Land.

Fig. 3. Northrop, Henry Davenport. *Treasures of the Bible: A Land Flowing with Milk and Honey.* 1894.

God was not pleased with them, and made them stay in the desert for 40 years. Forty years represented a typical lifespan. That time in the desert thus ensured that an entire generation of Israelites, who had come so close to the Promised Land, and yet turned away in fear, would die without ever entering.

Only two Israelites lived to see the plagues, leave Egypt, witness the parting of the Red Sea, *and* enter the land. Those two were Joshua and Caleb. God rewarded them for the great faith they had shown, even in the midst of overwhelming opposition and doubt.

The Faith of Rahab

At the beginning of Joshua, when the forty years were over, more spies entered the Promised Land and went to a great city called Jericho.

Jericho was notorious for its fortified walls and military garrison. These protected the people inside from all the threats that surrounded them, and made the name and the city of Jericho a formidable opponent. In normal circumstances, no sane person would even attempt to take this city without a large standing army, a well-defined battle plan, and a tolerance for heavy casualties.

But God had a better way of delivering Jericho to his people: by inspiring a person within the walls to lend aid. His choice may seem rather surprising to us, for when the spies arrived at Jericho, they discovered one person with faith in the Lord: a lowly prostitute, by the name of Rahab.

Rahab and her family had heard of Yahweh and his fearsome power, and believed, though no other person in the city did:

"'For we have heard how the LORD dried up the water
of the Red Sea before you when you came out of Egypt,
and what you did to the two kings of the Amorites
who were beyond the Jordan to Sihon and Og,
whom you devoted to destruction.
And as soon as we heard it, our hearts melted,
and there was no spirit left in any man because of you,
for the LORD your God,
he is God in the heavens above and on the earth beneath.
Now then, please swear to me by the LORD that,
as I have dealt kindly with you, you also will deal kindly with my father's house..."'
(Joshua 2:10-12)

The town guards then arrived at her house, which was just off the fortified wall. Rahab knew that the spies had to leave quickly and used a scarlet rope to lower them down to the outside of the wall. The spies agreed to spare Rahab and her family when the Israelites attacked Jericho.

Rahab was recognized for her faith in the Lord. She would marry an Israelite named Salmon and give birth to Boaz, one of the ancestors listed in Jesus' genealogy in the Gospel of Matthew. Though she was a Gentile, God brought her into the fold of his chosen people—just as he would in the fullness of time, through the cross.

Fig. 4. *Rahab and the Emissaries of Joshua.* Unknown Italian artist. 17th Century. Oil on canvas. Musée des Beaux-Arts de Nîmes.

The Threshold Moment

When the Israelites arrived at the River Jordan with the Ark of the Covenant, God granted them easy passage: he held back the waters, and the people were able to cross on dry land. It meant that, at long last, the people were prepared to cross the threshold that had held them back for forty years. Though crossing a river may seem rather a small miracle in comparison with the parting of the Red Sea, it was just as significant to the people of Israel—if not more significant.

As a reminder of God's covenant and providence, they took 12 memorial stones and set them on the bank. They would not forget the day that Joshua and the Israelites crossed the River Jordan and entered the Promised Land. And one day, in that same place, John the Baptist would baptize people, in a reenactment of Joshua's threshold moment on the river.

"And when the soles of the feet of the priests bearing the ark of the LORD, the Lord of all the earth, shall rest in the waters of the Jordan, the waters of the Jordan shall be cut off from flowing, and the waters coming down from above shall stand in one heap." (Joshua 3:13)

Fig. 5. West, Benjamin, *Joshua Passing the River Jordan with the Ark of the Covenant,* 1800.

As soon as they crossed the River Jordan, Joshua remembered the covenant that God made with Abraham. God had promised them this land. He had brought them in with his mighty hand. It was clear that God was delivering the land to them. What came next was vitally important: the people had to bring themselves fully into covenant with the Lord.

None of the men who had grown up in the wilderness had been circumcised. They were not ready to continue Abraham's legacy and live into the covenant the Lord had made with him. The solution was to hold a mass-circumcision. Collectively, their circumcisions would serve as a sign that they and their society were fully and uncompromisingly committed to Yahweh. It may seem an extreme, even fanatical, measure to modern readers, but such was the radical faith of the generation who had grown up in the wilderness. They were tough, and they were absolutely committed to the promises of God.

Unlike the generation before them, they had not known the comforts and luxuries of life in Egypt. The previous generation could and did look back (with rose-tinted lenses) to Egypt as a better life than the wilderness. As people sometimes do today, they also saw their romanticized past life more clearly than the future of a Promised Land, and this kept them from fully trusting in God rather than their own flawed memories.

But all the younger generation had ever known was the harsh wilderness. Thus, they only had a vision of the future to compare to the wilderness. The Promised Land offered them a vision of God's grace and love—and nothing else in their lives could even pretend to compare.

In Genesis, Creation began in the *tohu va bohu*, the formless void, and ended with Sabbath rest. What God did in the covenant with Moses was to create a new people, following the same arc as his original creation. Just as he had created the heavens and the earth and all that is in them, he created Israel out of wilderness and chaos, into Sabbath rest in a beautiful country of milk and honey.

The Battle of Jericho

After crossing the Jordan, the next task for the Israelites was to fight for the Promised Land, against the people who were already there. As Joshua surveyed Jericho in the middle of the night, he encountered the commander of the army of the Lord. However, he did not know who the commander was, and asked him whether he was for the Israelites or for the people of Jericho.

Fig. 6. Schönfeld, Johann Heinrich. *Battle of Jericho.* Before 1684. Oil on panel. Prague Castle Picture Gallery.

The commander simply responded that he was the leader of the army of the Lord, and ordered Joshua to take off his shoes, for he was standing on holy ground. And Joshua did so, because he knew that the commander was sent by God himself.

Through this, God reminded Joshua that the battle of Jericho was much larger than a mere skirmish between two nations. God is not a supporting character or a kingmaker who simply chooses the side he prefers among flawed human options. To use a modern example, he's not a registered Republican or Democrat. If he were, then human beings would have the power to dictate right and wrong! Instead, he is the ruler who asks the people to join *his* side, which transcends all others.

The Promised Land did not belong to the Hittites, or the Amorites, or the Jebusites, or the Anakites, or even the Israelites. It belonged (and belongs) to God. In fact, the whole earth belongs to him. But most people do not really understand the world this way. They believe that they own the piece of land in which they live; or, they claim that *their* god owns that piece of land—as if they owned or controlled their god.

But God is not owned or controlled by anybody—he is the creator and sole proprietor of all things, and anything we have, we hold in his trust. Thus, the only truly allegiance we have to consider is whether we will recognize and support God, the Lord of all.

After Joshua had affirmed that he was on God's side (and not the other way around), the commander told Joshua to march the Israelites around the walls of Jericho, blowing trumpets and carrying the Ark of the Covenant before them. They were to repeat this march every day. On the seventh day, after a long trumpet blast, the people of Israel would shout and the walls of Jericho would collapse.

Fig. 7. Doré, Gustave. *The Walls of Jericho Fall Down.* 1866. Doré's English Bible.

A more skeptical man might have questioned such an unlikely outcome. Marching around in circles was an unusual battle strategy, to say the least, and mighty walls did not tend to fall to the sound of trumpets, no matter how loud. But Joshua, a man of deep faith, trusted God to work great things through his people. And the people of that generation trusted in God as well, for when they heard God's plan, they were ready to go and do exactly what he had asked.

"...Joshua said to the people, 'Shout, for the LORD has given you the city. And the city and all that is within it shall be devoted to the Lord for destruction. Only Rahab the prostitute and all who are with her in her house shall live, because she hid the messengers whom we sent.'"
(Joshua 6:17)

DEVOTED TO DESTRUCTION: Under the Ban

The city of Jericho was totally corrupt and wicked. God said that the city and its people were "devoted to the Lord for destruction." Joshua and his men were to destroy the city and all of its inhabitants, with the sole exception of Rahab's household.

In 21st-century America, the notion of wiping out a city, and killing all of its men, women, and children, as well as its livestock and animals, is utterly abhorrent. The term "war crime" comes quickly to mind.

But life was quite different in the days of Joshua. In a country with an abundance of resources, survival comes rather easily, and physical violence appears unnecessary (and thus unjustifiable). There was no violence in the Garden of Eden, and there is rather little in the Western world today compared to its history. But even in the land of milk and honey, those resources were quite scarce relative to the ones much of the world enjoys today. People and nations would do battle against each other for what little there was, and the strongest would survive. Violence was a way of life.

One could argue, convincingly, that they would all have been better served in the long term by cooperating with each other and sharing what they had—one biblical example is found with Joseph seeing the pagans of Egypt through seven years of famine—but that would require more imagination, foresight, and goodwill than human beings are often inclined to show.

Sadly, much of the world still struggles with scarcity, and thus with widespread violence. Perversion, corruption, and brutality abound in these places. Likewise, the people of Jericho were regularly involved in rape, abuse, and barbarity. It was a matter of the strong dominating the weak—survival of the fittest.

If a society attempts to exist apart from God and his morality, it will break down into anarchy. In Sodom and Gomorrah, for example, a mob surrounds Lot's house and demands that the angelic guests staying with him be brought out for gang rape. Jericho was much the same as Sodom and Gomorrah, and along with the cities of Ai and Hazor, it was designated by God for destruction.

But even in this inherently violent land, God held the Israelites to a higher standard than the prevailing warrior culture. Though defeating enemies and removing threats was one goal of conquest, there was another one, which was at least as important—taking the spoils. Usually, conquerors would take women as wives, children as servants, and possessions, such as livestock and grain, as precious commodities. They became stronger at the expense of the weak.

But God wanted the Israelites to understand that their eventual strength would not be built upon the spoils of their enemies. Instead, that strength would come directly from the Lord. The Israelites were told to kill everyone—men, women and children. They were to destroy everything, including their houses, their possessions, their furniture, and their livestock. They were to take no plunder for personal gain, and anything of value, such as gold, was to be dedicated to the temple. They had to trust that God would provide them with everything they needed after the conquest was over.

Furthermore, God gave the Israelites directions not to destroy all of the tribes in the Promised Land. Some of them had been helpful and friendly to Abraham, according to Genesis, and God and the Israelites did not forget that kindness.

You may recall that, in his covenant with Abraham, God said, "I will bless those who bless you and him who dishonors you I will curse…."(Genesis 12: 3) Over those four or five hundred years of history, the tribes who had cursed Abraham continued as enemies to Israel, while the ones who were preserved and blessed in Joshua's time were the ones who had been friends to Abraham and his family. The conquering Israelites could remember the stories of how the ancestors of each tribe had treated their ancestors, and act accordingly. They would begin to learn the importance of mercy Thus, the neighboring peoples could all see God's covenant in action, and that their interactions with Israel could bring them great blessings—or great curses.

The Temptation of Looting

The Israelites strictly followed God's directions in Jericho, but in the city of Ai, one man looted some idols and household items for himself. Because the people were not fully trusting in God's providence, they stopped receiving his aid. Their conquests began to falter, and the Lord stopped speaking to the Joshua and the Israelites. They had assumed God was with them, but he was not anymore. They began to lose battles, and were only able to turn it around after removing the plunder in their midst, and once again fully trusting in God.

Stealing a few idols may not seem like a big deal, but it was a foothold for sin and pride within the Israelite camp. It would have led to more looting and encouraged the belief that the Israelites alone deserved full credit for their victories. If God had allowed it, then the entire endeavor of creating a holy nation would, over time, be compromised and ruined.

"There are devoted things in your midst, O Israel. You cannot stand before your enemies until you take away the devoted things from among you."
(Joshua 7:13)

Divide: Allocating Canaan

Once the land was successfully taken, the people had to determine how to allot it to the descendants of each of the 12 sons of Jacob: Reuben, Simeon, Levi, Judah, Issachar, Zebulun, Dan, Naphtali, Gad, Asher, Joseph, and Benjamin. The third section of the Book of Joshua explains how they divided the land.

There are a few quirks: the descendants of Levi are not allotted a specific portion of land because they instead serve as priests; they are known as the Levites. The number twelve is preserved by the splitting of Joseph's tribe in two, each tribe named after one of his two sons, Ephraim and Manasseh, respectively.

Map 1. *Map of the 12 Tribes.*

Small Compromises

Each of the tribes was called to conquer the land they had been assigned. Gad and Zebulun, for example, had to conquer particular areas and subdue them on their own. But the people of Israel did not drive out everyone. They compromised in some places:

"Yet the people of Israel did not drive out
the Geshurites or the Maacathites,
but Geshur and Maacath dwell
in the midst of Israel to this day."
(Joshua 13:13)

Joshua had managed to address a small compromise with the man who had looted idols. However, other small compromises, such as with Geshur and Maacath, began to occur, and this would cause big problems for the Israelites later on. Often, sin works not by causing people to dramatically abandon God all in one moment, but by encouraging them to take one small step at a time. People stray from the straight and narrow path just a little, and just a little more, until it is out of sight. The Israelites decided to save problems for later, and it would come back to haunt them.

In contrast, Caleb, Joseph's deputy and one of the original spies, had great faith. He was faithful to the Lord, and would not compromise.

He was assigned the area of Hebron, the same place where he had spied many years earlier and saw the giants known as the Nephilim. They were tough, entrenched, and mean. No one was interested in fighting them.

> "Verse 13 seems matter-of-fact enough; incomplete obedience usually is. It brings no immediate crisis. It seldom does. However, here is testimony to all God's people: We frequently and strangely prove faithful in great crises of faith, remain steadfast in severe storms, perhaps even relish the excitement of the heaviest assaults, yet lack the tenacity, the dogged endurance, the patient plodding often required in the prosaic affairs of believing life; we are often loathe to be faithful in (what we regard as) little."
>
> Dale Ralph Davis, Old Testament Scholar

But Caleb, who had clamored to take over the Promised Land in the days of Moses, was not afraid of them, and claimed that he could fight them just as well at 75 years old as he did when he was 30:

"I am still as strong today
as I was in the day that Moses sent me;
my strength now is as my strength was then,
for war and for going and coming.
So now give me this hill country
of which the LORD spoke on that day,
for you heard on that day how the Anakim were there,
with great fortified cities.
It may be that the LORD will be with me,
and I shall drive them out just as the LORD said."
(Joshua 14:11-12)

Land as Sabbath Rest:

Land is the locus of blessing

To be outside the land is exile and curse

The land is to be a holy land inhabited by a holy people

Unholy inhabitants defile the land with unholy worship and practice

Rest equates with the fulfillment of total possession and absence of war

God grants rest to those who are holy and committed to him

Rest is a gift

Land as Sabbath Rest

The fourth and final part of Joshua is about keeping the land. The Lord gave the Israelites rest from their enemies after they secured the land, and there was peace. Joshua brought the tribes together and created memorial stones with the law inscribed on them. He had a reading of the covenant of Moses before all the people.

"And the Lord gave them rest on every side
just as he had sworn to their fathers.
Not one of all their enemies had withstood them,
for the LORD had given all their enemies into their hands."
(Joshua 21:44)

Joshua also challenged the Israelites. They had a choice: they could serve God or serve the gods of Egypt or Amor. Joshua knew what he would do:

"And if it is evil in your eyes to serve the LORD, choose this day whom you will serve, whether the gods your fathers served in the region beyond the River, or the gods of the Amorites in whose land you dwell. But as for me and my house, we will serve the Lord."
(Joshua 24:15)

The Book of Joshua ends with the Israelites saying,

"The LORD our God we will serve and his voice we will obey."
(Joshua 24:24)

Sabbath Rest:
Earthly freedom from conflict
Eternal Life in the Presence of God

Eternal Life in the Presence of God

"For if Joshua had given them rest,
God would not have spoken of another day later on.
So then, there remains a Sabbath rest for the people of God,
for whoever has entered God's rest has also rested
from his works as God did from his.
Let us therefore strive to enter that rest,
so that no one may fall by the same sort of disobedience."
(Hebrews 4:8-11)

CHAPTER 5 NOTES:

CHAPTER 6
King: God's Anointed One

Objective: The maturing disciple of Jesus will understand the fundamental role of the monarchy and the Davidic Covenant for shalom—peace in the land.

JUDGES: Defending the Jewish monarchy

The book of Judges serves in large part as a defense of the Jewish monarchy. After the people commit to serving the Lord at the end of Joshua, they form a rather decentralized government. This causes issues to arise. The main one is that there is no single unifying figure like Joshua to keep them focused on the Lord. The three main sections of the book show Israel becoming more and more corrupt because of a general lack of faithfulness to God's word. While God raised several leaders, known as judges, to save and guide Israel, none of these provisional leaders kept the people faithful in a lasting way. Ultimately, it seemed, Israel needed (or wanted) an earthly king to uphold the authority of the divine king.

Faltering Conquests

"Be very careful, therefore, to love the LORD your God.
For if you turn back and cling to the remnant
of these nations remaining among you and make marriages with
them, so that you associate with them and they with you,
know for certain that the LORD your God
will no longer drive out these nations before you,
but they shall be a snare and a trap for you,
a whip on your sides and thorns in your eyes,
until you perish from off this good ground
that the LORD your God has given you."
(Joshua 23:11-13)

Problems and Weakness in the Land:

Remaining in the land requires obedience

The Israelites compromise and tolerate unfaithfulness

The Judges' sin, weakness an finiteness results in anarchy and depravity

Israel needs the order and stability that can only be provided by a king

The Book of Judges:

Faltering Conquests (1:1-3:6)

Cycles and Decline (3:7-16:31)

Anarchy and Depravity (17:1-21:25)

> **Yahweh Chaos to Sabbath Rest:**
>
> *In the same way Yahweh created everything, he is creating Israel*
>
> *The Word—God speaks and it comes to be*

In general, the book of Joshua has a positive perspective on the execution of the conquest of Canaan. But even Joshua himself is clear that the Israelites faltered, and at times failed to accomplish everything the Lord had asked of them.

The book of Judges begins with the success of the southern tribe of Judah in contending with the Canaanites in their allotted area. Crucially, Judges emphasizes the cooperation between Judah and its brother tribe Simeon: *"And Judah went with Simeon his brother"* (Judges 1:17). Although the Lord was with Judah, he *"could not drive out the inhabitants of the plain"* (Judges 1:19). However, when the tribes worked together, they succeeded to a larger extent than they otherwise would have.

For the northern tribes, conquest did not go particularly well either. Six of those tribes failed, in the same way as Judah, to drive out the inhabitants as God had commanded. Failings that seemed insignificant and minor at the time would prove to be a "thorn" in Israel's side and a "snare" to entrap them into idolatry:

> **The Land as Holy Sabbath Rest:**
>
> *The fourth commandment is to keep the Sabbath holy*
>
> *The tabernacle is where Yahweh places the footstool of his heavenly throne*
>
> *That which is abomination must be devoted to destruction*
>
> *Israel is to be a kingdom of priests*

"Now the angel of the LORD went up from Gilgal to Bochim.
And he said, 'I brought you up from Egypt
and brought you into the land that I swore to give to your fathers.
I said, "I will never break my covenant with you,
and you shall make no covenant with the inhabitants of this land;
you shall break down their altars."
But you have not obeyed my voice.
What is this you have done?
So now I say, I will not drive them out before you,
but they shall become thorns in your sides,
and their gods shall be a snare to you.'
As soon as the angel of the LORD spoke these words to all
the people of Israel,
the people lifted up their voices and wept."
(Judges 2:1-4)

Small Compromises Lead to Big Problems

The author of the book of Judges shows that a key problem was a failure in succession. Joshua and the generation who entered the land were "gathered to their fathers." They had seen firsthand the things the Lord had accomplished. The generation after them *"did not know the Lord or the work that he had done for Israel"* (Judges 2:10). Their lack of intimacy with the Lord set up a recurring cycle: first, they would fall into idolatry; then, God would pass judgment on them; they would call out to him in their distress, and he would deliver them through an anointed leader; and in a few years, they would fall back into ignorance, which would inevitably lead to idolatry.

The fact that God provided judges so many times shows his long-suffering nature and his compassion toward Israel. Time and again, the Lord *"saved them from the hand of their enemies"* and was *"moved to pity by their groaning"* (Judges 2:18). Unfortunately, the Israelites failed to recognize and appreciate God's love and patience for them, and their general trajectory under the judges' leadership was a downward spiral.

> *"But whenever the judge died,*
> *they turned back and were more corrupt than their fathers,*
> *going after other gods, serving them and bowing down to them.*
> *They did not drop any of their practices or their stubborn ways."*
> *(Judges 2:19)*

> *"They did not destroy the peoples,*
> *as the LORD commanded them,*
> *but they mixed with the nations and learned to do as they did.*
> *They served their idols, which became a snare to them.*
> *They sacrificed their sons and their daughters to the demons;*
> *they poured out innocent blood,*
> *the blood of their sons and daughters,*
> *whom they sacrificed to the idols of Canaan,*
> *and the land was polluted with blood.*
> *Thus they became unclean by their acts,*
> *and played the whore in their deeds.*
> *Then the anger of the LORD was kindled against his people,*
> *and he abhorred his heritage;*
> *he gave them into the hand of the nations,*
> *so that those who hated them ruled over them."*
> *(Psalm 106:34-41)*

The Cycle of Sin in Judges:
- Israel serves the Lord
- Israel falls into sin and idolatry
- Israel is enslaved
- Israel cries out to the Lord
- God raises up a Judge
- Israel is delivered

Baal Worship

In the days of Judges, most cultures had at least one god or goddess of sexual fertility. These deities would usually be sexually active, for it was through their sexuality that every living thing in the world was procreated and could procreate.

> **apostasy**—(noun)
> **apos·ta·sy \ ə-ˈpäs-tə-sē**
> an act of refusing to continue to follow, obey or recognize a religious faith
> *Merriam-Webster Dictionary*

This, of course, is not how Yahweh could be described. According to Genesis, the world did not come about through sex. Instead, Yahweh "spoke," and the creation and its goodness came into being and brought forth increase. God gave sex as a gift to creation, so that it could fulfill his command to *"be fruitful and multiply"* (Genesis 1:28); he himself does not partake as the pagan gods of fertility did. Like other conditions of human life, such as birth, death, gravity, and the passage of time, sex does not apply to God. Even in the Incarnation, when God the Son became a man subject to birth, death, gravity, and time, he was born *of a virgin*—a fact that some in the Church have found difficult to accept, even today.

A Creator who was not sexual was also difficult for the Israelites to accept, for their very existence, and the existence of all living things around them, was tied to sex. Wouldn't it make more sense to say that everything was originally created through divine sex? That was, after all, what the Canaanites believed about their god Baal. Now, *there* was a god that made sense to the Israelites!

Baal was the Canaanite god of fertility and storms. He was, in many ways, the opposite of Yahweh: he would have sex all the time with his female consort, the goddess Ashtoreth (or Ashtart)—a veritable obsession for the Canaanites. And Baal insisted that the people worship him through temple prostitution and child sacrifice—two practices that were utterly abhorrent to Yahweh. Like most pagan gods, Baal was, for all intents and purposes, a human being with superpowers, and, as an idol, seemed more concrete, relatable, and comprehensible than the invisible, all-powerful, unfathomable Yahweh. Whenever the Israelites strayed from the Lord, they tended to gravitate towards Baal and other gods like him.

Their recurring idolatrous worship and practice became a snare to the Israelites as they intermarried with the Canaanites. The nation of Israel was called to be distinct from paganism, but intermarriage and idolatry blurred that distinction. Through not consciously endeavoring to remain godly, the people developed a sort of spiritual amnesia, slowly forgetting what it even meant to be godly. This spiritual amnesia eventually led to apostasy—a problem that the Church has always struggled with and continues to experience today.

CYCLES OF DECLINE AND SALVATION UNDER THE JUDGES

The middle section of the book of Judges focuses on the cycle of sin and salvation: Israel sins, Yahweh disciplines, Israel cries, Yahweh forgives. But the cycle has a general downward trajectory, because each time that God raises a new judge, that judge proves to be more incapable than the last of keeping Israel focused on serving the Lord. As a result, the Israelites stray further and further from God, despite the best efforts of their judges.

In "The New Laymen's Bible Commentary," Carl Armerding provides a helpful summary of this section of the book: "The first five judges, all of whom, including the mysterious Shamgar, were deliverer figures, represent a time when the land enjoyed rest from conflict .... (see Judges 3:11, 30; 5:31; 8:29) In contrast, the latter period is characterized by minor judges ... together with the rather unorthodox deliverers Jephthah and Sampson. The land is never said to have rest and the picture is one of increasing moral, political and military decline leading to the shameful climax of events in the epilogue (Judges 17-21)."

The two lessons from this repeated experience are clear: first, a people who fail to give wholehearted obedience to the Lord can only sink lower and lower; and second, the judges cannot fulfill Israel's desperate need for rule and administration.

Anarchy and Depravity

The author equates the lack of a central political authority with the lack of a central moral authority. The people, who clearly would not stay loyal to God of their own volition, were determining right and wrong for themselves, rather than following what God had given them in the Torah. Without the presence of a king, no one had the necessary authority or power to enforce God's law among a people inclined to stray from their Lord. The result, in short, was moral and political anarchy—a situation that was without a doubt abhorrent to God. This is a steady refrain in the last several chapters of Judges, which make explicit Israel's need for a king anointed by Yahweh's.

Micah the Idolater

The first episode of Israel's gradual breakdown is the story of Micah. Though his mother, a God-fearing woman, had said, *"Blessed be my son by the Lord,"* (Judges 17:2) Micah turned his back on God, setting up a household of idols and establishing a private priesthood to serve them. He celebrated when a Levite came to his personal shrine, and believed (wrongly, of course) that it was a sign that Yahweh was blessing his deeds!

But Micah was not blessed for his idolatry, and through it, the people of Israel strayed further from God. The tribe of Dan, which was

The Salvation of Yahweh
(Judges 3:7-16:31)

The Paradigm of Yahweh's Salvation
(Othniel, 3:7-11)

The Excitement of Yahweh's Salvation
(Ehud and Deborah, 3:12-5:31)

The Weakness of Yahweh's Salvation
(Gideon, 6:1-8:32)

The Antithesis of Yahweh's Salvation
(Abimelech, 8:33-9:57)

The Strangeness of Yahweh's Salvation
(Jephthah, Sampson 10:1-16:31)

Davis, Dale Ralph. "Such a Great Salvation, Expositions of the Book of Judges."

Fig. 1. Slide 6.

looking for a place to settle, traveled through Ephraim and stayed at Micah's house. Spying his many idols, the Danites decided to rob him, conquer the nearby city of Laish, and rename it Dan. After they settled, they and their priests worshipped a particularly valuable idol that Micah had made of silver, *"as long as the house of God was at Shiloh."* (Judges 18:31)

This kind of evil could only occur because every man did what was right in his own eyes. Micah and the Danites would have stayed in right relationship to God if only a godly king were around to ensure it.

"If the LORD of hosts had not left us a few survivors,
we should have been like Sodom,
and become like Gomorrah."
(Isaiah 1:9)

The Levite and His Concubine

The next story is about a Levite and his concubine—a fact which alone showed how people largely made their own rules in those days! The account bears eerie similarities to the attempted gang rape in Sodom and Gomorrah: when the Levite and his concubine stayed with an old man in the city of Gibeah, the men of the city, "worthless fellows," surrounded the house and demanded that the old man hand the Levite to them so that they might know him. The man refused, instead forcing his guest's concubine outside, where she was raped all night and left to die. When the Levite found her body, he cut her up into twelve pieces and sent them to all the tribes of Israel, so that they would understand the outrageous barbarity that had occurred.

The acts of all involved showed just how depraved the Levites and other Jewish tribes had become without Yahweh's kingly rule. When the people learned what happened, they were shocked and began to consider how such a thing could occur:

"And all who saw it said,
'Such a thing has never happened
or been seen from the day that the people of Israel
came up out of the land of Egypt until this day;
consider it, take counsel, and speak.'"
(Judges 19:30)

Self-Destruction and Self-Provision

The entire assembly of the tribes then came together to determine what they needed to do about the evils and the depravity in their midst. They concluded, correctly, that their problems were largely internal in nature; however, rather than seeking repentance, Israel turned against itself. The city of Gibeah, where the men had raped the Levite's concubine, belonged to the tribe of Benjamin. When the other tribes demanded that Benjamin hand over the wicked men of Gibeah, Benjamin refused. The tribes then fought against the men of Benjamin, putting 25,000 of their men of valor to the sword. It was a tragic and devastating civil war.

The tribe of Benjamin was decimated as a consequence of its anarchy. Only a handful of men survived the battle. The other tribes, who had already sworn an oath not to give their own daughters in marriage to Benjamin, took pity on the tribe (which was, despite everything, one of the 12) and considered how to ensure they would not entirely disappear. The men needed wives, so the tribes went to the city of Jabesh-gilead and killed all its inhabitants except for 400 young virgins, whom they handed over to Benjamin. For the remaining men, they told them to kidnap women from Shiloh who went to dance during the yearly feast of the Lord.

None of these events would have occurred if the people of Israel had stayed faithful to the Lord—no killing, no kidnapping, no war. The events of Judges showed the need for a new political and moral system, which would crack down on the depravity and insanity that dominated in those generations and bring Israel back into right relationship with God.

The final verse thus serves as a short, simple, and stinging indictment of the dark days before the monarchy:

"In those days there was no king in Israel.
Everyone did what was right in his own eyes."
(Judges 21:25)

A KING LIKE OTHER NATIONS

The books of 1 and 2 Samuel then show us what happens when Israel gets its king. Israel had grown weary of the judges, and wanted a king to judge them "like all the nations" (1 Samuel 8:5). In the end, God would give them Saul as king, and then, when Saul turned away from the Lord, David would take his place. The central goal of the books of Samuel was to encourage Israel to have faith in David's descendants, though David was a flawed king.

Structure of 1, 2 Samuel:

Foundation of the Kingdom
(1 Samuel 1-7)

Saul's Kingdom (1 Samuel 8-15)

David's Kingdom
(1 Samuel 16-2 Samuel 20)

Future of the Kingdom
(2 Samuel 21-24)

Foundation of the Kingdom

The prophet Samuel was the last judge over Israel. To the Israelites, the future of the system seemed bleak, for Samuel's sons Joel and Abijah, were corrupt and greedy. The people of Israel knew that a leadership crisis would come when Samuel died, and they wanted a permanent solution:

*"The all the elders of Israel gathered together
and came to Samuel at Ramah and said to him,
'Behold, you are old and your sons do not walk in your ways.
Now appoint for us a king to judge us like all the nations.'
But the thing displeased Samuel when they said,
'Give us a king to judge us.'
And Samuel prayed to the LORD."
(1 Samuel 8:4-6)*

Samuel did not want to give Israel a king. He saw it as a rejection of him and his rule, in which he had tried to serve the Lord faithfully. Like Moses before him, he pleaded with the Lord for Israel, for he knew that God was the only true king. But God told his prophet that it was not their judge the Israelites were rejecting; it was their God. The Lord chose to grant the people their wish, and not to force them to follow him; all he asked was that Samuel warn them about the true nature of earthly kings.

Samuel told the people who their king would be. He would be a tyrant, who would control their lives and tax their belongings, and they would be his slaves. One day, they would cry out against the tyrant they had chosen, but the Lord would not answer them in that day. They would surely not want a king if they truly understood what they were asking.

Fig. 2. Guercino. *Saul Attacking David.* 1646. Oil on canvas. Galleria Nazionale d'Arte Antica, Rome.

But the people would not listen to Samuel:

*"'No! But there shall be a king over us,
that we also may be like all the nations,
and that our king may judge us
and go out before us and fight our battles.'"
(1 Samuel 8:19-20)*

110 Old Covenant and Ancient Israel

God had set Israel apart from all the other nations. The book of Judges was correct: like the other nations, Israel *did* need a king; but the king they needed was not a man. They needed only to recognize the Lord their God as their true King. But on that sad day, the Israelites chose sameness over holiness and human rule over divine sovereignty. Soon, much as Esau had traded his birthright for a bowl of soup, they would trade their freedom for temporary security, their responsibility for permanent dependence, and the blessing of the Lord for the curse of tyranny.

Saul's Kingdom

*"And he had a son whose name was Saul,
a handsome young man. There was not a man among the people
of Israel more handsome than he. From his shoulders upward he
was taller than any of the people."*
(1 Samuel 9:2)

The Lord chose Saul, of the tribe of Benjamin, as king. He was a tall, handsome man who had the look of a great and mighty king. However, if one looked beyond Saul's physique to his soul, he would see a deep insecurity, which would one day be his undoing. The people, whose criteria for leadership were quite superficial, valued Saul's outward appearance of strength, but did not recognize his inner failing: *"Do you see him whom the LORD has chosen? There is none like him among all the people. ... 'Long live the king!'"* (1 Samuel 10:24). Truly he was a king like the kings of other nations.

From early on, a few men saw the great expectations placed upon the new king's shoulders, and doubted that he could live up to them. Though they are described as "worthless" for causing trouble, they asked, rather astutely, *"How can this man save us?"* (1 Samuel 10:27) It would prove to be a question for which Saul had no answer.

United Kingdom:

Saul: *A King Like Other Nations*
(1 Samuel 9-31)

David: *A Man after God's Heart*
(2 Samuel 1-24)

Solomon: *The King of Peace*
(1 Kings 1-11)

The Rise of David and the Fall of Saul

Samuel was right about the people. When he gave a farewell address, the people, who remembered his just reign, quickly saw the errors of their ways. They asked Samuel:

*"Pray for your servants to the LORD your God,
that we may not die,
for we have added to all our sins this evil,*

CHAPTER 6 King: God's Anointed One 111

to ask for ourselves a king."
(1 Samuel 12:19)

Samuel assured them that God will not abandon them or their king, so long as they served his will. However, Saul proved to be a rash and ill-suited leader for his people, who cared too much about what the people thought of him and not enough about what God thought. The Lord rejected him as king over Israel and announced to Samuel that he had chosen a new king, a son of Jesse of Bethlehem, from the tribe of Judah.

When Saul was anointed, the text focused on his stature and appearance. He was *"taller than any of the people from his shoulders upward"* (1 Samuel 10:23). However, his outward appearance masked the deep insecurity of his self-hiding.

With the new king, the criteria were different. When Samuel traveled to Bethlehem to anoint the new king, he believed at first that Eliab, the handsome oldest son, was God's chosen. But the Lord said:

> *"'Do not look on his appearance or on the height of his stature, because I have rejected him.*
> *For the LORD sees not as man sees:*
> *man looks on the outward appearance,*
> *but the Lord looks on the heart."*
> *(1 Samuel 16:7)*

Samuel listened carefully to the Lord, who rejected Jesse's seven oldest sons. Surprisingly, it was the youngest son, David, who received the divine appointment. Samuel was faithful to the voice: *"Arise, anoint him, for this is he"* (1 Samuel 16:12). The outward sign of Samuel anointing David with oil accompanied the inward grace of God filling David with the Holy Spirit:

> *"Then Samuel took the horn of oil and anointed him in the midst of his brothers. And the Spirit of the LORD rushed upon David from that day forward."*
> *(1 Samuel 16:13)*

Rise of David and Fall of Saul:

David's Success and Troubles in Saul's Service
(1 Samuel 16:1-18:30)

David's Anointing by Samuel
(1 Samuel 16:1-23)

David's Help as He Flees from Saul
(1 Samuel 19:1-22:5)

David's Innocence and Saul's Guilt
(1 Samuel 22:6-2 Samuel 1:27)

The Reign of King David

David quickly became a prominent figure in Israel, killing the giant Philistine Goliath who had taunted Israel for so long. Saul was jealous of David's fame, which soon overshadowed his own:

"And the women sang to one another as they celebrated,
'Saul has struck down his thousands,
and David his ten thousands.'"
(1 Samuel 18:7)

But God was on David's side, and protected him even through the many times that Saul tried to kill him. When Saul died, David was the obvious choice to succeed him.

The second book of Samuel focuses on David's reign. The book begins with David lamenting the death of his predecessor, and it ends with his last words (2 Samuel 23:1-7).

When David ascended to the throne, he only ruled over his own tribe of Judah; by the end of his life, he was king over a united kingdom of all Israel, as a priestly king. One of the keys to understanding 2 Samuel is in David's last words comparing the just ruler to worthless men. David's house stands or falls depending on the king's personal relationship with Yahweh and *"ruling in the fear of God"* (1 Samuel 23:3).

Fig. 3. Bernini, Gian Lorenzo. *David.* 1623-1624. Carrara marble. Galleria Borghese, Rome.

The Davidic Covenant

David, realizing that his own home was nicer than the tent in which the Ark of the Covenant abided, decided to build a "house" for the Ark of the Covenant. But God, through his prophet Nathan, told the king that he was not interested in a house built by David. Rather, it was David's house that would be built by Yahweh. The Lord made an everlasting covenant with David:

"And I will give you rest from all your enemies.
Moreover, the LORD declares to you that the Lord will make you a house.
When your days are fulfilled and you lie down with your fathers,
I will raise up your offspring after you,
who shall come from your body,
and I will establish his kingdom.
He shall build a house for my name,
and I will establish the throne of his kingdom forever.

Reign of King David (2 Samuel 2-24):

David's Rise to Power in Judah (2:1-4:12)

David's Rule over Israel (5:1-9:13)

David's Downfall into Sin (10:1-12:31)

Like Father, Like Sons (13:1-19:40)

One Nation under Yahweh (19:41-24:25)

> **Key Points of the Davidic Covenant:**
>
> *David's son is the Son of God*
>
> *He will build a house for Yahweh*
>
> *His throne will be eternal*

I will be to him a father, and he shall be to me a son.
When he commits iniquity, I will discipline him with the rod of men,
with the stripes of the sons of men,
but my steadfast love will not depart from him,
as I took it from Saul, whom I put away from before you.
And your house and your kingdom shall be made sure forever before me.
Your throne shall be established forever."
(2 Samuel 7:11-16)

The house of David was thus permanent established as royalty, upon an everlasting throne. His son, the wise Solomon, would be the one to fulfill David's dream of building a dwelling place for the Lord—the great Temple. The adoption of David and his heirs as "sons of God" would culminate in his descendant Jesus, the only-begotten Son of God and the ultimate temple builder.

David ruled in strength over all his enemies, for the Lord was on his side. He administered justice and equity over all Israel, and even showed kindness and loyalty to the house of his predecessor, Saul.

David's Fall into Sin

"It happened, late one afternoon,
when David arose from his couch
and was walking on the roof of the king's house,
that he saw from the roof a woman bathing;
and the woman was very beautiful.
And David sent and inquired about the woman.
And one said, 'Is not this Bathsheba, the daughter of Eliam,
the wife of Uriah the Hittite?'
So David sent messengers and took her,
and she came to him, and he lay with her.
(Now she had been purifying herself from her uncleanness.)
Then she returned to her house.
And the woman conceived,
and she sent and told David, 'I am pregnant.'"
(2 Samuel 11:2-5)

Fig. 4. Caravaggio. *David and Goliath.* 1599. Oil on canvas. Museo del Prado, Madrid.

Later in David's reign, the Israelites waged war against their neighbors, the Ammonites. David stayed in Jerusalem during the war, which provided the occasion for David to reveal a major flaw in his character—namely, the flaw of great lust. David coveted Bathsheba, the beautiful wife of his soldier Uriah. 2 Samuel may, depending on one's interpretation, imply either that David raped her, or that it was adultery on her part; regardless, he committed great sin against Uriah, Bathsheba, and, of course, against the Lord. After leaving her with child, David tried to cover up his sin by calling for Uriah to return home and sleep with his wife, so that he would believe the child was his. But Uriah's honor would not permit him to leave his duty.

"Uriah said to David, 'The ark and Israel and Judah dwell in booths, and my lord Joab and the servants of my lord are camping in the open field. Shall I then go to my house, to eat and to drink and to lie with my wife? As you live, and as your soul lives, I will not do this thing.'"
(2 Samuel 11:11)

Fig. 5. Gentileschi, Artemisia. ***Bathsheba.*** c. 1636-1637. Oil on canvas. Columbus Museum of Art.

Out of options, David decided to have Uriah killed. He sent Uriah to the front line of battle, where his death was a near-guarantee. When Uriah was killed, David took Bathsheba to be his own wife. Unsurprisingly, the conduct of the king greatly *"displeased the Lord"* (2 Samuel 11:27). David, whom God had chosen to be righteous and faithful where Saul had been wicked and selfish, had coveted another man's wife, committed adultery (and possibly rape), and murdered a man. That means that David disobeyed three out of the Ten Commandments—arguably an even worse record than that of his predecessor.

The Confrontation

History shows us that it is a very dangerous prospect to challenge a king for his misdeeds. King James, who commissioned the first official Bible in English, once argued that just as it was blasphemy to question God, so it was sedition to question the king that God had appointed over a realm. God's representative on earth could very well execute anyone who did so.

Would anyone dare to confront David about his egregious sins? Only if God were on their side. The Lord gave his prophet Nathan great wisdom and courage before the king. Nathan came to David and told him a story about a rich man who took advantage of a poor man. David felt outrage against the rich man, but he did not see the hypocrisy of his own words and actions. As Jesus might say, he saw the speck in another man's eye, but not the log in his own.

"Nathan said to David, 'You are the man!
Thus says the LORD, the God of Israel, I anointed you king over Israel, and I delivered you out of the hand of Saul.
And I gave you your master's house and your master's wives into your arms and gave you the house of Israel and of Judah.
And if this were too little, I would add to you as much more.
Why have you despised the word of the LORD, to do what is evil in his sight? You have struck down Uriah the Hittite with the sword and have taken his wife to be your wife and have killed him with the sword of the Ammonites. Now therefore the sword shall never depart from your house, because you have despised me and have taken the wife of Uriah the Hittite to be your wife."
(2 Samuel 12:7-10)

Fig. 6. Tissot, James. *David Dances Before the Ark.* 1896-1902. Gouache on board. Jewish Museum, New York.

David finally saw his sin, and he understood how deeply he had offended the Lord, who had given him so much. He repented of that sin in part by writing Psalm 51, in which he prayed: *"Have mercy on me, O God, according to your steadfast love; according to your abundant mercy blot out my transgressions."* (Psalm 51:1) And God kept David on the throne, in accordance with his promise of an eternal throne. However, David's sin had grave consequences: the son he conceived with Bathsheba died seven days into his young life, and the house of David would for many generations be associated with lust and violence.

In time, though, the Lord would give David and Bathsheba another son, Solomon. He would become the heir to the throne. Nathan called him Jedidiah, or "beloved of the Lord," because the Lord loved him.

David's rule was, on balance, a good period for Israel; he was usually merciful, pardoning his enemies, and he managed to bring the entire nation under his just and gracious rule—no small feat considering the civil wars of Judges, which would still have been in living memory for many. However, his personal sin proved costly for him and his descendants, and for Israel. To be a good leader under Yahweh requires faithfulness—even more than David showed.

KINGS, KINGS AND MORE KINGS

The books of 1 and 2 Kings were completed sometime after the exile in Babylon. The Israelites, far from home and in bondage under the Babylonians, certainly struggled over their suffering outside the Promised Land. Why had Yahweh allowed Israel, his chosen people, to fall to its enemies? Where was the Lord in the midst of their misery? How could he permit the destruction of the temple?

The truth was that, as Samuel had prophetically warned the people, earthly kings would prove to be a curse rather than a blessing to the Israelites. Because many of these kings were themselves prone to worship other gods, they would lead the people astray as well. Just as the book of Judges had shown that the people of Israel needed a king, the failures of the kings of Israel showed that the king they truly needed was the King of Kings, Jesus Christ.

1 and 2 Kings show how, over several generations, Israel, united under David and Solomon, split into a northern and a southern kingdom. Both kingdoms gradually strayed further and further from God and were eventually overrun by their external foes. Assyria captured Israel in 722 BC. Judah fell to the Babylonians in 586 BC. As Yahweh repeatedly warned through his prophets, the covenant he had made with his people went both ways: they needed to be faithful on their end to receive the blessing of prosperity and peace in the Promised Land.

Structure of 1 Kings and 2 Kings:

A United Kingdom: Solomon
(1 Kings 1-11)

A Divided Kingdom
(1 Kings 12-2 Kings 9)

The Fall of the Northern Kingdom: Israel (2 Kings 10-17)

The Fall of the Southern Kingdom: Judah (2 Kings 18-25)]

A UNITED KINGDOM: Solomon

The seeds of Israel's downfall as a nation state under Yahweh were sown in the days of glory. The height of Israel's power and fame was under David and Solomon. According to some calculations, Solomon was the richest man who has ever lived, wealthier in today's terms even than Bill Gates or John D. Rockefeller. However, the sins of these leaders led to deep internal divisions. David's sin with Bathsheba and Solomon's worship of gods other than Yahweh would contribute to the Lord's severe judgment upon the kingdom.

Solomon's Power and Wealth

"And now, O LORD my God,
you have made your servant king in place of David my father, although I am but a little child.
I do not know how to go out or come in.
And your servant is in the midst of your people whom you have chosen,
a great people, too many to be numbered or counted for multitude.
Give your servant therefore an understanding mind to govern your people, that I may discern between good and evil,
for who is able to govern this your great people?"
(1 Kings 3:7-9)

Fig. 7. Poussin, Nicolas. *The Judgment of Solomon.* 1649. Oil on canvas. Musée du Louvre, Paris.

God was pleased when Solomon, at the beginning of his reign, asked him for wisdom, when he could have asked for wealth or long life. He grants his prayer and gives him riches and honor to match his great wisdom. Everything that Yahweh had promised Abraham was now being fulfilled in Solomon's kingdom—blessing, greatness, international influence and land.

118 Old Covenant and Ancient Israel

"And people of all nations came to hear the wisdom of Solomon, and from all the kings of the earth, who had heard of his wisdom."
(1 Kings 4:34)

The House of the Lord

"Then he called for Solomon his son
and charged him to build a house for the LORD, the God of Israel.
David said to Solomon, 'My son, I had it in my heart
to build a house to the name of the LORD my God.
But the word of the LORD came to me, saying,
"You have shed much blood and have waged great wars.
You shall not build a house to my name,
because you have shed so much blood before me on the earth.
Behold, a son shall be born to you who shall be a man of rest.
I will give him rest from all his surrounding enemies.
For his name shall be Solomon,
and I will give peace and quiet to Israel in his days.
He shall build a house for my name.
He shall be my son, and I will be his father,
and I will establish his royal throne in Israel forever."'"
(1 Chronicles 22:6-10)

As you may recall, when David decided to build a temple for the Lord, Nathan told him that his son Solomon would be the one to build it.

Solomon's plan for the temple was elaborate and would require resources and expertise from faraway lands. Thankfully, his father had had a good friend: Hiram, the king of Tyre (in present-day Lebanon) and a skilled Gentile craftsman. Hiram was only too happy to help Solomon, and provided cedar and other materials that would go into much of the temple and its furniture. He also formed an extensive workforce of laborers in Israel.

The construction project took seven years to complete. The descriptions of the temple were elaborate and designed to show the glory of God. But 1 Kings mentions that as the temple was being completed, Solomon also commissioned the construction of his own glorious home, as well as his throne and a house for his Egyptian wife. This is where Solomon began to take the blessing of God for granted and gave way to hubris.

*"Now the word of the LORD came to Solomon,
'Concerning this house that you are building,
if you will walk in my statutes and obey my rules
and keep all my commandments and walk in them,
then I will establish my word with you,
which I spoke to David your father.
And I will dwell among the children of Israel
and will not forsake my people Israel.'"*
(1 Kings 6:11-13)

*"Let your eyes be open to the plea of your servant
and to the plea of your people Israel,
giving ear to them whenever they call to you."*
(1 Kings 8:52)

Temple Completion and Dedication

Once the temple was completed, the Ark of the Covenant was brought into the Holy of Holies. Yahweh remained faithful to his word and filled the house with his glory:

*Then the priests brought the ark of the covenant of the LORD
to its place in the inner sanctuary of the house,
in the Most Holy Place, underneath the wings of the cherubim.
For the cherubim spread out their wings over the place of the ark,
so that the cherubim overshadowed the ark and its poles....*

*And when the priests came out of the Holy Place,
a cloud filled the house of the LORD,
so that the priests could not stand to minister because of the cloud,
for the glory of the LORD filled the house of the LORD."*
(1 Kings 8:6-7, 10-11)

Solomon gave a blessing for the Lord and the people. He then offered a sevenfold prayer of dedication to God. He prayed, above all, that the temple would be a place for individuals and the nations of the world to commune with the one true God of heaven. Solomon prayed that the Lord would hear and forgive those who came to the temple with a spirit of repentance and petition.

There has never been as elaborate a dedication and celebration to

Yahweh as the feat Solomon held: the people offered 22,000 oxen and 120,000 sheep to the Lord. It was a joyous and blessed occasion for all!

"On the eighth day he sent the people away, and they blessed the king and went to their homes joyful and glad of heart for all the goodness that the LORD had shown to David his servant and to Israel his people."
(1 Kings 8:66)

The Downfall of Solomon

God reminded Solomon that everything that Solomon asked of him has come to pass. God confirmed and renewed the covenant he had made with David by charging Solomon to remain faithful to the stipulations. Yahweh told Solomon that if the king walked in Yahweh's ways, *"then I will establish your royal throne over Israel forever"* (1 Kings 9:5). If, however, the king were to turn from the Lord's command and serve other gods…

Fig. 8. Platzer, Johann Georg. *The Temple of Solomon in Jerusalem.* 1700s. Oil on copper. Private collection.

"I will cut off Israel from the land I have given them,
and the house I have consecrated for my name
I will cast out of my sight ....
And this house will become a heap of ruins."
(1 Kings 9:7-8)

This warning would prove all too prescient. Solomon's own words from his dedication prayer—*"for there is no one who does not sin"* (1 Kings 8:46)—included him and would show that the people could not and would not uphold the covenant.

The book of Deuteronomy anticipated the possibility that Israel might one day establish a king, and laid out specific guidelines for that future king:

"Only he [the King] must not acquire many horses for himself
or cause the people to return to Egypt in order to acquire many horses,
since the LORD has said to you, 'You shall never return that way again.'
And he shall not acquire many wives for himself, lest his heart turn away,
nor shall he acquire for himself excessive silver and gold."
(Deuteronomy 17:16-17)

Solomon would depart from all of these commands. He hoarded gold, traded horses with Egypt and took foreign wives (700 of them, along with 300 concubines!) The foreign wives would prove to be his downfall in his relationship with the Lord: they would lead him to build temples to false gods, and his heart turned to them over time: "his wives turned away his heart after other gods" (1 Kings 11:4). The consequences of Solomon's sins would play out in the rest of Kings.

"Now King Solomon loved many foreign women, along with the daughter of Pharaoh: Moabite, Ammonite, Edomite, Sidonian, and Hittite women, from the nations concerning which the LORD had said to the people of Israel, 'You shall not enter into marriage with them, neither shall they with you, for surely they will turn away your heart after their gods.' Solomon clung to these in love. He had 700 wives, who were princesses, and 300 concubines. And his wives turned away his heart. For when Solomon was old his wives turned away his heart after other gods, and his heart was not wholly true to the LORD his God, as was the heart of David his father."
(1 Kings 11:1-4)

Fig. 9. Ghiberti, Lorenzo. ***Solomon and the Queen of Sheba.*** 1425-1452. Gilded bronze. Baptistry, Florence.

In following generations, the Lord in his anger would remove his hand of protection from Solomon's kingdom by raising adversaries from the north and the south and even within his own nation. The prophet Ahijah prophesied to one of Solomon's adversaries, Jeroboam:

"And he said to Jeroboam, 'Take for yourself ten pieces, for thus says the LORD, the God of Israel, "Behold, I am about to tear the kingdom from the hand of Solomon and will give you ten tribes (but he shall have one tribe, for the sake of my servant David and for the sake of Jerusalem, the city that I have chosen out of all the tribes of Israel), because they have forsaken me and worshiped Ashtoreth the goddess of the Sidonians, Chemosh the god of Moab, and Milcom the god of the Ammonites, and they have not walked in my ways, doing what is right in my sight and keeping my statutes and my rules, as David his father did."'"
(1 Kings 11:31-33)

*"Why do the nations rage
and the peoples plot in vain?
The kings of the earth set themselves,
and the rulers take counsel together,
against the LORD and against his Anointed, saying
'Let us burst their bonds apart
and cast away their cords from us.'*

*He who sits in the heavens laughs;
the LORD holds them in derision.
Then he will speak to them in his wrath,
and terrify them in his fury, saying,
'As for me, I have set my King
on Zion, my holy hill.'*

*I will tell of the decree:
The LORD said to me, 'You are my Son;
today I have begotten you.
Ask of me, and I will make the nations your heritage,
and the ends of the earth your possession.
You should break them with a rod of iron
and dash them in pieces like a potter's vessel.'*

*Now therefore, O kings, be wise;
be warned, O rulers of the earth.
Serve the LORD with fear,
and rejoice with trembling.
Kiss the Son,
lest he be angry, and you perish in the way,
for his wrath is quickly kindled.
Blessed are all who take refuge in him."*
(Psalm 2)

The story of Israel's kings covers about 300 years. Throughout those years, the rulers demonstrated certain patterns of behavior including reformation, repentance, apostasy, sin and loss. Mostly, they continually turned away from the Lord their God, to worship false idols of other peoples and things of this world. Lessons for us all to remember.

CHAPTER 6 NOTES:

CHAPTER 7
Prophets: Repent and Be Redeemed

Objective: The maturing disciple of Jesus??

When God sent his prophet Ahijah to Jeroboam, Ahijah tore 12 pieces of cloth from his cloak and gave 10 of them to Jeroboam. This symbolized the separation of the twelve tribes of Israel: God would tear most of the kingdom away from Solomon's heir, Rehoboam, and give them to Jeroboam. Only the southern tribes of Judah and Benjamin remained loyal to the House of David—which made its prospects for the future rather bleak. Even in the midst of this disunity, the Lord had not forgotten the promise he made to David that his kingdom and his throne would stand forever (2 Samuel 7:16), for the Messiah would come through David's family line.

THE DIVIDED KINGDOM: Rehoboam and Jeroboam

1 Kings 12 marks this defining moment for Israel. After Solomon's death, the people of the kingdom came out to meet their new king, Rehoboam. They had been unhappy with Solomon's reign, and believed that the change in leadership was an opportunity to bring about reform. They pleaded with Rehoboam, *"Your father made our yoke heavy. Now therefore lighten the hard service of your father and his heavy yoke on us, and we will serve you."* (1 Kings 12:4). Little did Rehoboam know that this plea was not a request, but an ultimatum, for the people were prepared to serve Jeroboam if Rehoboam did not do as they asked.

Knowing that this decision would define the rest of his reign, Rehoboam asked the people to give him three days to consider their plea. To be sure, it was a difficult decision: granting their request might make him appear weak and force him to make further concessions later. Denying it risked rebellion. He asked several advisers for counsel, and there were several conflicting opinions.

It seems that Rehoboam did not inherit his father's legendary wisdom, for he listened to bad advisers and made the worst possible decision. When he emerged from his palace, he told the people, *"My little finger is thicker than my father's thighs. And now, whereas my father laid on you a heavy yoke, I will add to your yoke. My father disciplined you with whips, but I will discipline you with scorpions."* (1 Kings 12:10-11).

God had directly warned King Solomon not to turn to other gods, but Solomon would not listen. (1 Kings 11:11) When given the opportunity to change course, Rehoboam doubled down on his father's strategy. God would not bless Rehoboam's arrogance, and the ten tribes would soon leave.

Divided Kingdom, Immediate Decline

When Jeroboam took the 10 tribes in the northern part of the kingdom (Asher, Dan, Ephraim, Gad, Issachar, Manasseh, Naphtali, Reuben, Simeon, and Zebulun), God warned Rehoboam to let them go (1 Kings 12:24). Rehoboam, who had learned the hard way that "pride goes before destruction, and a haughty spirit before a fall," (Proverbs 16:18) decided to listen this time and quietly went home to Jerusalem, in Judah.

Fig. 1. Crispin van den-Broeck. *Ezekiel and the Dry Bones.* 16th century.

In Samaria, Jeroboam began to create a new government. The biggest challenge before him was the Temple in Jerusalem. He knew that faithful Jews would want to return to their old capital and sacrifice to God. That was not ideal, because it meant that Rehoboam would still have a certain amount of power and authority over the ten tribes.

To solve this problem, it seems that Jeroboam took inspiration from Aaron: he set up his own altar and made two golden calves! And when he told the people, *"Behold your gods, O Israel, who brought you up out of Egypt,"* (1 Kings 12:28) they were only too happy to comply.

Though Jeroboam had been chosen by God, he decided to lead his people astray. In addition to idols, he established festivals and ordained priests that God had not authorized. The new kingdom was even more sinful than the old one. And this apostasy continued for centuries!

Division of the Kingdoms in 930 BC

Northern Kingdom: Israel

- *Dominant Tribe: Ephraim (Sometimes the whole nation is referred to by this name.)*
- *Capital City: Samaria*
- *First King: Jeroboam (God chose him, but he did not honor God, 1 Kings 13:33-34)*
- *History of Kings: All of the kings of Israel were evil. Not one did right before God.*
- *Year Conquered: 722 BC*
- *Destroyed by: the Assyrians*

Southern Kingdom: Judah

- *Dominant Tribe: Judah*
- *Capital City: Jerusalem*
- *First King: Rehoboam*
- *History of Kings: Few good kings, but most were bad. Some do good for most of their reign, but sin at some point.*
- *Year Conquered: 586 BC*
- *Conquered by: Nebuchadnezzar, King of Babylon*

Map. 1. *The Divided Kingdom.*

The Three Messianic Offices

The kingdoms of Israel and Judah desperately needed redemption for their sins. Thankfully, the Lord provides, and he told his prophets that he would in due time send them a Messiah to save his beloved people from themselves.

Messiah means *anointed one*. In the Bible, to anoint someone with oil was to show that Yahweh had set him apart for a special role. For instance, when God chose David to be king, Samuel anointed him with oil. He was a messiah of sorts, but the Messiah who would redeem Israel and the world would come much later, after the kingdoms gave way to one foreign empire after another.

Until that time came, God instituted a three-part system, calling some to be priests, others to be prophets, and still others to be kings. All of these people were chosen by God, and their offices were messianic in that sense.

The Levite priesthood, an order that began with Aaron, were the descendants of Levi. Their tribe was considered the priestly tribe. Even those Levites who were not priests still served the temple in some capacity. God set strict laws for how this tribe was to behave (Leviticus 21). Priests also served as judges for the people, and the High Priest could make judgments that the whole nation was to follow (Numbers 27:21). Because they did not own land, they were spread out among both kingdoms and were not counted as one of the twelve tribes.

Kings were called by God to lead the nation. They were sometimes called as "sons of God;" this is not to be understood literally, but as an indicator of a unique relationship with the Lord (2 Samuel 7:14, Psalm 89:26). When a man became king, he was supposed to write and keep with him a copy of the entire law. He was to study it every day (Deuteronomy 17:18). Kings were never to lead by their own will, but by God's will.

Finally, the prophets identified and authorized the kings as God's witness, and did their best to keep them in right relationship with the Lord. As God's ambassadors, the prophets were advisers and prosecutors for his covenant with Moses, mediating the blessings and curses that came from obeying (or disobeying) the laws their ancestors had sworn to uphold. If a king began to stray, God would speak through the prophet to keep him in line. Often, the prophets held their kings accountable for specific sins, as Nathan did for David after his shameful conduct with Bathsheba.

Three Messianic Offices:
Prophet

Priest

King

THE ROLE OF THE PROPHET: Covenant Advisers, Prosecutors, Compasses and Accountability Holders

Many of the kings were more interested in the prophets' gift of predicting whether they would win an upcoming battle. After all, the prophets knew what God wanted! If there was a battle to be fought, the king would ask the prophets: "Should we go up in battle against this enemy?" And it was the prophet's job to say: "Yes, the Lord is with you," or "No, this is a bad idea." The kings did not always accept the prophets' recommendations, but whenever they did not, it would lead to disaster. The prophets were the kings' moral compass.

> **Box with Role of the Prophet:**
>
> *Provided compass and accountability*
>
> *Covenant Advisor: Is Yahweh with us or not?*
>
> *Covenant Prosecutor: Pronounced blessings and curses*

The books of Kings frequently used the phrases "He walked in the sight of the Lord" or "He did evil in the sight of the Lord" to summarize each king's rule. Sadly, most of the kings earned the latter designation; only a few, like Josiah and Hezekiah, cared about serving the Lord. If a king was wicked, there would be a series of consequences: a crop failure might lead to the death of a king's family member, or a loss in battle, until God finally removed his protection and provision and allowed for enemies and internal division to bring down the proud and stubborn king.

"He did evil in the sight of the Lord."

How to Tell a Good King from a Bad King

In the Bible, it is fairly easy to tell a good king from a bad king. It is usually summarized somewhere at the beginning or end of their story. Here are some examples:

__2 Chronicles 31:20:__ Thus Hezekiah did throughout all Judah, he did what was good and right and faithful before the Lord his God.

__2 Kings 15:1-4:__ In the twenty-seventh year of Jeroboam king of Israel, Azariah the son of Amaziah, king of Judah, began to reign. He was sixteen years old when he began to reign, and he reigned fifty-two years in Jerusalem. His mother's name was Jecoliah of Jerusalem. And he did what was right in the eyes of the Lord, according to all that his father Amaziah had done.

__1 Kings 22:51-53:__ Ahaziah ... reigned two years over Israel. He did what was evil in the sight of the Lord and walked in the way of [those] who made Israel to sin. He served Baal and worshiped him and provoked the Lord, the God of Israel, to anger in every way that his father had done.

But the prophets would always warn the king first. Most kings did not listen to the warnings, and the ultimate consequence for the kingdoms of Israel and Judah were destruction and exile. The monarchy was supposed to save the people from the violence and chaos of time of the judges, but the kings were no less sinful than their people. The wicked Northern Kingdom would fall to the Assyrians in 722 BC, while the slightly less wicked Southern Kingdom would hold

Kings & Prophets from Split to Captivity

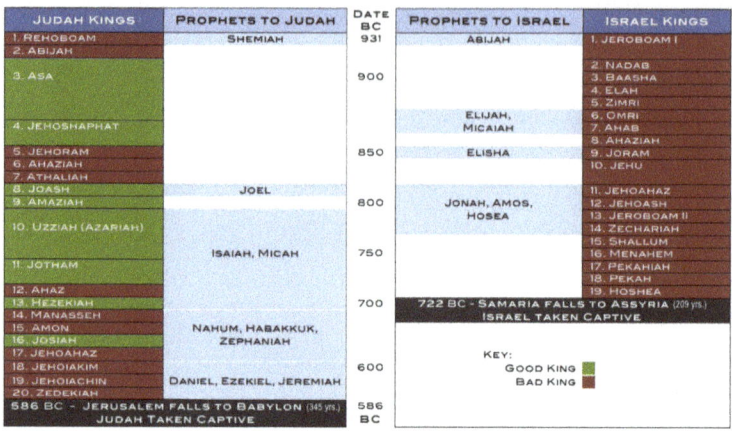

Fig. 2.

Map. 2.

out about another 150 years, only to fall to the Babylonians in 586 BC. When the people rejected God as their true king, they would lose their land and end up back in exile.

The ultimate consequence for not keeping God's covenant was returning to the life their nation had before they made it.

Prophets to other nations

Israel and Judah were not the only nations that needed to heed God's will! The prophets also spoke to the rulers of other nations, who brought continuous threats and battles to the people of Israel, and God gave warnings to those nations through the prophets. Jonah, for example, was told by God to prophesy annihilation to the wicked city of Nineveh, which then repented and was ultimately spared.

Yahweh is the true God of all nations, whether they recognize him or not. God loves all of them, and holds all of them accountable to uphold justice, peace and godliness. Everyone who blessed Israel would be blessed, because Israel was God's hand of blessing in the world—and everyone who cursed it would be cursed.

Israel's role was to bless the other nations of the world, so that they would look to Israel's God and Messiah for direction, leadership and salvation. And this would happen from time to time: Rahab the prostitute was crucial to Joshua's conquest of Jericho. Ruth, a Gentile woman, chose to serve God rather than leave her mother-in-law Naomi. Naaman, a commander in the Syrian army, renounced his god Rimmon and proclaimed Yahweh as Lord after being cured of leprosy in the River Jordan. But until Jesus came, these conversions were isolated events, and not the salvation of all nations.

Here a map of nations around Israel. May need more than one, as territory changed hands during the divided kingdom. For length, including all in one would be easiest (but maybe historically inaccurate?)

132 Old Covenant and Ancient Israel

LITERARY STRUCTURE: The Major and Minor Prophets

Most prophets prophesied orally, but several of them, known as the "writing prophets," also wrote down their words. Theologians often refer to Isaiah, Jeremiah and Ezekiel as the "major prophets," not because they were more important than others like Habakkuk or Micah, but because their writings were large enough to require their own scroll. The minor prophets' writings are all 14 chapters or less—the shortest, Obadiah's prophecy, is only one chapter long—and usually shared scrolls.

Form of Prophetic Literature

The prophets describe similar beginnings to their ministry. First, a prophet must be called by God. Isaiah described his call in Chapter 6: *"In the year that King Uzziah died I saw the Lord sitting upon a throne, high and lifted up; and the train of his robe filled the temple."* (Isaiah 6:1). When the Lord asked who would go and speak for him, Isaiah volunteered. He told God that he was unworthy, as a man of unclean lips from a people of unclean lips, so God sent a seraph to purify his mouth and make him worthy to be God's mouthpiece. Isaiah explained this story to show his authority. He did not prophesy by his own will; he was called by God to be his ambassador.

The Call

The first prophet to be called in this way was Moses (though earlier non-prophetic figures such as Noah and Abraham also received callings from God). When God appeared to Moses in the form of a burning bush, Moses was afraid and reluctant to accept the call. But when the time came to lead the people out of Egypt, and to receive God's law for them, Moses was the only one who would go, because God himself sent him.

Why did the people of Israel listen to Moses? Because he was the only one who would go up on the mountain and speak face to face with God. Likewise, the major and minor Prophets had each accepted a special call from the Lord; and by that call, the people knew that they were not to be ignored.

Fig. 3. Giovanni Battista Tiepolo. *The Prophet Isaiah.*

The Prophetic Track Record

Along with divine sanction, the prophets had an obvious way of establishing their credibility: they only predicted events that actually came to pass! Moses' Law advised the people on this point:

"...when a prophet speaks in the name of the LORD,
if the word does not come to pass or come true,
that is a word that the LORD has not spoken;
the prophet has spoken it presumptuously.
You need not be afraid of him."
(Deuteronomy 18:22)

To ensure that Judah would heed his words, Isaiah reminded them about the prophecies he had made about the Northern Kingdom before writing the book of Isaiah. He had warned them that they would be conquered by the mighty Assyrian Empire. In 722 BC, it happened, just as he had said. The people of Judah, therefore, needed to take what he would say very seriously.

The Message of Judgment

The prophets, by grounding their message in their callings and their records, would then proceed to proclaim what God had said to them. In Chapter 28, Isaiah proclaimed that Judah would fall, just as Israel had fallen. All who had taken refuge in lies would find no safe place from the wrath of God (Deuteronomy 28:15). His judgment would be swift and just. God had shown himself as the true King of Israel when he rescued the nation from slavery in Egypt, provided for them, gave them a law and a land. By disobeying Yahweh's law and rejecting him as king, the people had sealed their fate. They would end as they began: slaves living in a foreign nation, far from their homes.

> **Key Elements of Judgment:**
> *Wicked and Deceitful Nature of Man*
> *Departure of the Lord's Presence*
> *Withdrawal of the Lord's Protection*
> *Invasion and Exile*

Prophecies of judgment were very simply structured, reminiscent in some ways of a trial. They would begin a call to attention, usually indicated by the word "woe." Next would come the charges against the people for specific violations of the law, which included hoarding wealth, not caring for the poor, overindulgence, sexual immorality, idolatry, corruption, and turning against God. Sometimes, the prophets would even call witnesses, so that there would be no doubt of the people's guilt. When that guilt was established, the prophets would pronounce God's judgment upon them.

The Message of Restoration

However, many of the prophets do not end with judgment. Isaiah also prophesied restoration: one day, the Lord would raise up a "redeemer" who would allow a remnant from Judah to return home and rebuild the city of Jerusalem. This redeemer would prove to be King Cyrus of Persia. In the same way, Ezekiel prophesied against the nations who had been enemies of Israel, he also prophesied hope.

The Fall of Samaria

From the beginning of division, the northern kingdom of Israel did evil in the sight of the Lord by worshipping idols, setting up various forms of false worship, hoarding wealth, and generally living however they liked. Israel's kings were constantly shunning God's messengers and inventing new evil practices, and there was not a single good king among the 19 of them. Isaiah had warned them to turn away from their sin, as did Elijah, Joel, Amos, Hosea, and others. They never listened.

In 740 BC, God allowed the Assyrians to come in and start taking Israel's people from the land (1 Chronicles 5:26). And by 722 BC, Samaria was completely destroyed (2 Kings 17:5-6).

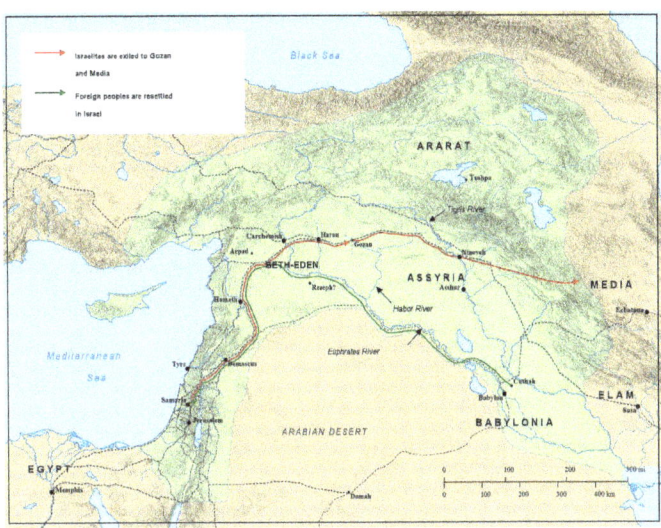

Map. 3. Map. *Fall of Samaria.*

The Nation of Judah would also fall, but because some of the kings of Judah did good in the eyes of the Lord, their destruction was delayed. The sin of Israel was so great that it had hastened their judgment, and made the kingdom's fall swift. It should have been a potent warning for Judah and Jerusalem.

The Multiple Applications of Old Testament Prophecy

"But do not overlook
this one fact, beloved,
that with the Lord
one day is as a thousand years,
and a thousand years as one day."
(2 Peter 3:8)

When people read these prophecies, it can be difficult for them to remember that God brings things about in his time, not in human time. The prophecies have both a time-sensitive message, intended for a contemporary audience, and a subtler message, which might only be better understood in later generations. Some prophecies were meant specifically for a certain king of Israel or Judah, or even another king or enemy nation. Others spoke of the coming of Jesus Christ, who in his birth, life, death, resurrection, and ascension, fulfilled more than 300 Old Testament prophecies. These parallel messages can make reading and interpreting the Prophets quite a challenge.

Some of the prophecies discuss the end of the world, including the final judgment and restoration of humanity. As Christians, knowing how deeply broken our world is, and how radically different it should be, we long for that day when Satan and his followers are finally vanquished and Christ guides us to a better home, a New Heaven and a New Earth.

The prophets of the Old Testament (and the New Testament) held out this great hope. Their words stand as warnings to all earthly and spiritual authorities who dare oppose the will of God—their days are numbered. But to the poor, oppressed, persecuted, and outcast people of God, the prophets preach encouragement, and promise new and eternal life in God for those who trust him.

It does not feel natural to most human beings to be patient. The Jews could not count the years until Messiah would come, just as we cannot count the years until he returns (Mark 13:32, Matthew 24:36-44). But what we do know is that Scripture told us that the Messiah would come not once, but twice. Jesus died for our sins and conquered death while he was on Earth, but there is yet more to come, as Jesus himself told his disciples at the Last Supper (John 14:1-3). Messiah's first appearing was to provide a solution for sin; the second will be to reign in his kingdom forever.

God is never late in fulfilling his promises: he sent Jesus at just the right time (Romans 5:6, Galatians 4:4), and his return will be just as timely:

"The Lord is not slow
to fulfill his promise
as some count slowness,
but is patient toward you,
not wishing that any should perish,
but that all should reach repentance."
(2 Peter 3:9)

The Contingent Nature of Prophecy

Then the word of the Lord came to me. He said, "Can I not do with you, Israel, as this potter does?" declares the Lord.

"Then the word of the LORD came to me: 'O house of Israel, can I not do with you as this potter has done? declares the LORD.

Behold, like the clay in the potter's hand, so are you in my hand, O house of Israel. If at any time I declare concerning a nation or a kingdom, that I will pluck up and break down and destroy it, and if that nation, concerning which I have spoken, turns from its evil, I will relent of the disaster that I intended to do to it. And if at any time I declare concerning a nation or a kingdom that I will build and plant it, and if it does evil in my sight, not listening to my voice, then I will relent of the good that I had intended to do to it.'"
(Jeremiah 18:5-10)

There is a contingent nature to the messages of the prophets. Many people think the prophets spoke, and it was done, that God was issuing his judgment, and it could not be stopped. But God first (and repeatedly) sent the prophets to warn kings – and even people who were not his people (like the Assyrians in Nineveh). The purpose was to motivate them to change their behavior, to repent.

The foretold future was contingent on their response to the prophecy. And there were degrees of judgment and degrees of blessing that would come with each message, based on the degree of obedience. This was what the law prescribed. Punishment could be delayed by temporary obedience, and blessings would pour in for full obedience. The prophecy was more a communication from a father than an edict from a king. (See Deuteronomy 28.)

If you compare Judah and Israel, you see that Israel, because it did nothing but evil from the start, fell sooner. Faithfulness actually delays judgment. Judah's fall was more than 100 years later. There were some good kings and some national repentance. And God held back their enemies then. This is a biblical principle.

Messianic Prophecies

All of the prophets had in common a sad but unavoidable conclusion: the heart of man, consumed by sin, was wicked and deceitful. There existed no covenant that could heal it, no law that could control it, no human solution that could stand against it. This conclusion is terrifying, for it means that we are not in full control of how good we are. The people in the time of the prophets refused to see the truth; they considered themselves holy because they had the temple of the Lord in Jerusalem. But Jeremiah warned them:

"Do not trust in these deceptive words:
'This is the temple of the LORD,

Key Promises of the New Covenant:

Yahweh would return as a messianic king

Suffering servant would atone for our sins

Forgiveness of sins

Resurrect his people and put his spirit within them

the temple of the LORD,
the temple of the LORD."'
(Jeremiah 7:4)

In fact, the glory of God was about to depart from the temple. God took up his chariot and left the temple and Jerusalem behind (Ezekiel 8-11). And when God's chariot departed from the temple, so did God's protection. Ezekiel's story of wheels and cherubim is not merely a children's story to be sung about (though many of us have learned it as a song). It is the tragic story of God leaving a people who had long ago left him in their hearts.

Fig. 4. Circle of Juan de la Corte. *The Burning of Jerusalem by Neb.*

The Fall of Jerusalem

With the temple and the city of Jerusalem unprotected, the fearsome empire of Babylon would come in and quickly destroy both. In 596, Nebuchadnezzar of Babylon laid siege on Jerusalem. He took their kings, their strong young men, their noble and educated class, all but the poorest of the land to exile in Babylon. Within 10 years, the entire capital city, the wall protecting the perimeter of the city and even the temple, had been looted and destroyed. This is a story of devastating national disaster at a level most of us cannot comprehend, but it all started with human hearts.

The Exile and the Return

The people of the Kingdom of Israel had been taken away and scattered. (They are now often referred to as the 10 lost tribes of Israel). The people of Jerusalem were taken into captivity in Babylon. But God did not leave them alone there. The prophets Jeremiah and Ezekiel wrote messages to encourage the exiles. Daniel was taken to Babylon in the first deportation from Jerusalem, and his prophecy was written from there. We will learn more about these prophets, the exiles in Babylon and their return to rebuild Jerusalem in the next chapter.

Incurable Sin and the Messages of Hope

"Woe is me because of my hurt!
My wound is grievous.
But I said, "Truly this is an affliction,

and I must bear it."'"
(Jeremiah 10:19)

"The heart is deceitful above all things,
and desperately sick;
who can understand it?"
(Jeremiah 17:9)

The Apostle Paul says that sin is so terrible that it can take God's good law and use it to arouse sin in us we would never have thought of on our own (Romans 7:8). The problem is not rooted in the law, but in our enslavement to sin (Romans 7:14), and no one can free an enslaved people except a Savior. We need a Savior who can provide for our forgiveness and give us new start.

Reducing the population to a few righteous people would not work. Neither would the elaborate sacrificial system laid out in the law to cover sin (Leviticus 4-7). This system was insufficient, because it could only pay for specific sins, temporarily, until they were committed again. The sacrificial system was a reminder of sins, not a cure for them. And the truth was that the blood of animals could never fully remove the weight of sin in any case (Hebrews 10:3-4).

The Only Solution

"I will sprinkle clean water on you, and you shall be clean from all your uncleannesses, and from all your idols. I will cleanse you. And I will give you a new heart, and a new spirit I will put within you. And I will remove the heart of stone from your flesh and give you a heart of flesh. And I will put my Spirit within you, and cause you to walk in my statutes.... And I will deliver you from all your uncleannesses."
Ezekiel 36:25-29

"I will give them a heart to know that I am the LORD, and they shall be my people and I will be their God, for they shall return to me with their whole heart."
(Jeremiah 24:7)

Jeremiah and Ezekiel both present the only possible solution for this scattered people and the sick and sinful heart of humankind: complete forgiveness, a new heart, and a new covenant promise, all

Born Again

Nicodemus was a Pharisee (John 3). He had worked to earn the highest level of righteousness a man could earn in first century Judaism. When Jesus told him he needed to be "born again," he made clear that no level of human-earned righteousness could ever be enough to save a man from sin. In fact, righteousness that we believe we've earned or achieved by our own self-will can become a hindrance to true salvation from sin (Isaiah 57:12, 64:6, Romans 10:3). Jesus told Nicodemus that he had to be *"born again."*

achieved by God's amazing grace. Jeremiah 31 tells the story of God's great rescue and restoration. God would conquer those who had conquered them; he would gather his people and restore them. This extravagantly loving and exceedingly gentle shepherd (Jeremiah 31) would write his laws on their hearts and fill their minds with them. And these people with hearts and minds full of God's Word would become his: "I will be their God, and they shall be my people" (Ezekiel 37:27). All people, from the least to the greatest, would know him, and they would be a pure people, because he would remember their sins no more. (Jeremiah 31:31-34).

But, in order for this to happen, the matter of sin had to be addressed. Someone had to pay the price for all of it; this someone would be his beloved and chosen One (Isaiah 42:1), the joy of his heart (Matthew 12:18).

Isaiah foretold some of what the Messiah would undergo: he would suffer our punishment and die on a cross, and endure the contempt of men through it all. He would be pierced by man and crushed by the One who loved him the most. His undeserved punishment would bring us peace, and his terrible wounds would heal us. Quietly he would submit to torture and death, and no one would try to prevent it (Isaiah 53).

> **Prophecies of Blessing:**
>
> *Appeal to Attention*
>
> *Announcement of Blessing*
>
> *Call to Faithfulness*
>
> *Promises and Descriptions of Blessings*

Fig. 5. Crispin van den-Broeck. *Ezekiel and The-Dry Bones.* 16th century.

Restoration

But God promised restoration too. God called Ezekiel to prophesy to a valley full of bones. The bones were a stark reminder that Israel could not save itself, and that its people would not live forever. Surprisingly, God told Ezekiel to speak to the bones, to tell them that he would put his spirit in them. Ezekiel did as God asks, though he no doubt looked crazy doing it. The Lord called to him, *"Prophesy to the breath; prophesy, son of man, and say … come from the four winds, O breath, and breathe on these slain, that they may live."* (Ezekiel 37:9). And miraculously, they get up and formed a great army.

There is no limit to the Messiah's power, even to raise the dead to new life. He would grow into a righteous branch from the tree of David, and become king (Jeremiah 23:5-6), just as God had promised David long ago (2 Samuel 7:16). He would reign wisely and do only right. And this pure and perfect King would rule forever:

"Then the seventh angel blew his trumpet,
 and there were loud voices in heaven, saying,
"The kingdom of the world
has become the kingdom
of our Lord and of his Christ,
and he shall reign forever and ever.""
(Revelation 11:15)

CHAPTER 7 NOTES:

CHAPTER 8
Restoration: Exile and Return

Objective: The maturing disciple of Jesus will understand the promise of restoration from exile and the challenges restoration brings.

DANIEL: A Spirit of Excellence

"And the king spoke with them,
and among all of them none was found like Daniel,
Hananiah, Mishael, and Azariah.
Therefore they stood before the king.
And in every matter of wisdom and understanding
about which the king inquired of them,
he found them ten times better
than all the magicians and enchanters that were
in all his kingdom."
(Daniel 1:19-20)

Fig. 1. Rubens, Peter Paul. *Daniel in the Lion's Den.* c. 1615. Oil on canvas. National Gallery of Art, Washington.

God, always in Control

After the fall of the kingdom of Judah, the Israelites spent many years in exile. They were brought to Babylon to live under the direct reign of King Nebuchadnezzar. It was a time of great pain and sadness for the people, whom God had sent away from the Promised Land, the only home they knew as a free people.

But God was not finished with them. Even in exile, he raised a prophet named Daniel who, like Joseph before him, would rise to prominence through the interpretation of a king's dream! Daniel, whose name means "God is my judge," was the author and main character of the book of Daniel. A Jewish exile who had been taken in the first deportation, during the reign of King Jehoiakim (609-597 B.C.), he was a member of the Babylonian royal court under both Nebuchadnezzar and his successor, Belshazzar; and when Babylon eventually fell to the Medo-Persian Empire, Daniel served the governor of the region, Darius the Mede.

Daniel's personal ministry spanned two empires and almost 70 years, but his visions and prophecies extended even further, covering four major empires and culminating in the arrival of the Messiah and the final conflict at the end of time.

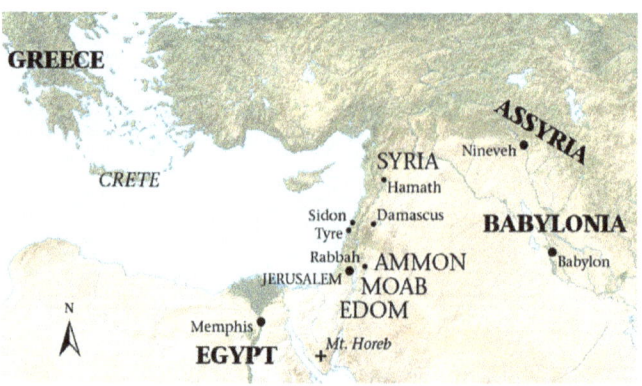

Map.1. *Map of the fall of Samaria and Jerusalem.*

The book of Daniel, a complex and multifaceted text, was written in two different languages. The first chapter, the second half of chapter 7, and the entirety of the final five chapters are in Hebrew, the language of the Jews. But chapters 2 through 6, as well as the first part of chapter 7, are written in Aramaic, the *lingua franca* of that time. Some Biblical scholars explain this unusual feature by arguing that the passages in Hebrew were messages intended specifically for the Jews, while the Aramaic passages were intended for a broader audience—which might mirror the Gospels in each being written for different groups of Christians.

Chapters 1 through 6 of Daniel are in the form of a narrative, telling the story of Daniel's interpretation of dreams and visions and his rise to power within the court of the Babylonian king. The second half of the book describes four visions that Daniel received, which were then interpreted by the angel Gabriel.

The "hinge" chapter is chapter 7, in which Daniel receives the vision of the Ancient of Days and sees a being *"one like a son of man....And to him was given dominion and glory and a kingdom, that all peoples, nations and languages should serve him;"* (Daniel 7:13-14). It is fitting that chapter 7 is at the center of the book, as it provides the unifying theme for all of Daniel's seemingly unconnected parts.

Through the visions, God gave Daniel a glimpse of what lies behind the curtain of history and world events. The battles in which the empires and kings of this world fight are a microcosm of a larger war, a war waged on a spiritual battlefield between the very forces of good and evil. But the Lord is in control of all nations and in all situations, including the rise and fall of great empires. Kings can make plans all they want, but the Ancient of Days and his anointed king, the "son of man," rule over everything.

Literary Structure of the Book of Daniel:

Concentric Structure Establishing God's Sovereignty over Gentile Empires

Visions Given to Daniel

Shape of a Prophetic Lawsuit:

Call to Attention: Woe!

Announcement of Judgment

Charges, Specific Violations

Calling of Witnesses

Consequences

God is Sovereign over Gentile Empires

The first half of the book discusses Daniel and his three Jewish companions, Hananiah, Mishael, and Azariah. Ashpenaz, the king's chief eunuch, brought these four men into the royal court and gave them the names Belteshazzar, Shadrach, Meshach, and Abednego, respectively, which were to replace their Hebrew names. Over time, these men would rise to prominence in the Babylonian and Persian courts by being truthful advisors of integrity, faithful to God.

One day, the Babylonian king, Nebuchadnezzar, gave an impossible task to the wise men in his land: they were to interpret a dream that he had had—after telling *him* what that dream was! They told him that no one could do what he asked—how could they possibly know a dream they had not themselves had?

The king saw them all for who they were—charlatans—and ordered all the wise men of Babylon killed, which would have included Daniel and his friends. But with the revelation of God, Daniel was able to describe the dream and provide its interpretation before the king's order was executed.

Nebuchadnezzar's dream, as it turned out, was of a formidable statue. The statue had a golden head, silver chest and arms, bronze middle and thighs, legs of iron, and feet of iron and clay. Each of those medals represented an empire; Babylon was the golden head and would be followed by three other, lesser empires, culminating finally in a kingdom of iron and clay, partly strong and partly weak. They would all eventually be blown away by the wind, to be replaced by *"a stone cut from a mountain by no human hand,"* which would fill the earth and remain forever (Daniel 2:45). This stone, which would bring about an eternal kingdom built not on earthly riches but on a permanent foundation, is Jesus Christ, bringing to us the glorious kingdom of God.

Fig. 3. Aertsen, Pieter. *Worship of the Statue of Nebuchadnezzar.* c. 1552-60. Oil on panel. Museum Boijmans Van Beuningen, Rotterdam, Netherlands.

But it seems that the king cared far more about his short-lived kingdom of gold than God's eternal kingdom of stone. With no apparent sense of irony, Nebuchadnezzar commissioned a golden statue of himself, and ordered his subjects to worship it. Daniel's companions Shadrach, Meshach, and Abednego refused to worship the image, which led to their being thrown into a fiery furnace. Their commitment to worshipping the Lord mattered more to them than their own lives. And Nebuchadnezzar would begin to see that only the Lord truly held the power of life and death over his servants. To his surprise, they were not consumed by the fire, and they were joined by a mysterious fourth man:

Fig. 4. van Rijn, Rembrandt. *Belshazzar's Feast.* c. 1636. Oil on canvas. National Gallery, London.

"Then King Nebuchadnezzar was astonished and rose up in haste. He declared to his counselors, 'Did we not cast three men bound into the fire?' They answered and said to the king, 'True, O king.' He answered and said, 'But I see four men unbound, walking in the midst of the fire, and they are not hurt; and the appearance of the fourth is like a son of the gods.'"
(Daniel 3:24-25)

God protected Shadrach, Meshach, and Abednego from the most powerful man on Earth. And he was with them in that furnace. Nebuchadnezzar was to be humbled yet further by the Lord: he temporarily lost his sanity and lived as an animal. In the end, however, he finally acknowledged the source of all his power:

"At the end of the days I, Nebuchadnezzar, lifted my eyes to heaven,
and my reason returned to me, and I blessed the Most High,
and praised and honored him who lives forever,
for his dominion is an everlasting dominion,
and his kingdom endures from generation to generation;
all the inhabitants of the earth are accounted as nothing,
and he does according to his will among the host of heaven
and among the inhabitants of the earth;
and none can stay his hand or say to him, 'What have you done?'"
(Daniel 4:34-35)

Nebuchadnezzar's song of praise was a clarion call to all kings and rulers who would dare to set themselves higher than the king of Heaven. This included his successor, Belshazzar, who also proved an arrogant king. At a royal banquet, a disembodied hand began to write a message of doom on the wall, which David interpreted for his king. That night, Belshazzar was killed, and the empire fell to the Medes and Persians. This passage is the origin of the expression, "reading the writing on the wall," a warning of one's imminent downfall. Both kings arrogantly tested the sovereignty of the Lord, and both paid dearly for that arrogance.

In Chapter 6, Daniel bore witness to true faith in Yahweh when he chose to brave the lions' den rather than stop praying to the Lord. God once again showed his supremacy over the king by protecting Daniel from the hungry and ferocious lions, who were unnaturally peaceful in the presence of fresh meat!

Daniel and his friends showed to the Israelites that, while in exile, they needed above all to trust in the Lord. The pressure to compromise would be intense, but God would use his servants to humble kings, and the saints of God would triumph, with his help.

"And when he had said these things, as they were looking on,
he was lifted up, and a cloud took him out of their sight.
And while they were gazing into heaven as he went, behold,
two men stood by them in white robes, and said,
'Men of Galilee, why do you stand looking into heaven?
This Jesus, who was taken up from you into heaven,
will come in the same way as you saw him go into heaven.'"
(Acts 1:10-11)

The Ancient of Days and the Son of Man

The ultimate purpose of relating these memorable and eye-catching accounts is revealed in chapter 7. This chapter is resonant both theologically and thematically with the chapters that come before and after it within the entire book, and it brings them together.

In a vision, Daniel saw four terrifying beasts. These beasts were strange and complex: for example, Daniel saw a lion with eagles' wings, which then stood on two feet and had the mind of a man! The passage may seem cryptic at first blush; however, most interpreters see a connection to the four metals of the statue in Nebuchadnezzar's dream, which they believe correspond to the Babylonian, Persian, Greek, and Roman empires that precede the Kingdom of God.

But the power that ruled over all the beasts was the Ancient of Days—God. The Ancient of Days killed the fourth beast, which had iron teeth and ten horns, but allowed the others to live, for a time. He then brings about the ascent of the *"one like a son of man:"*

Four Beasts and Four Empires:

Babylonian

Persian

Greek

Roman

One Like a Son of Man

"I saw in the night visions, and behold, with the clouds of heaven there came one like a son of man, and he came to the Ancient of Days and was presented before him. And to him was given dominion and glory and a kingdom, that all peoples, nations, and languages should serve him; his dominion is an everlasting dominion, which shall not pass away, and his kingdom one that shall not be destroyed."
(Daniel 7:13-14)

Daniel was greatly concerned with the fourth beast, which was a vision not only of Rome but of an enemy of God and his people. The remainder of the book turns to this theme.

The Visions of Daniel

Daniel recorded three more visions in the final chapters. These visions, apocalyptic in nature, were interpreted by Gabriel, the Angel of the Lord, for *"the time of the end"* (Daniel 8:17). When Jesus arrived, it would be the end of the world as they knew it.

In chapter 8, Daniel saw a ram with two horns which conquered the beasts before it, until a mighty goat came and broke off its horns, conquering even more than the ram had. The angel explained that the ram with two horns was the Medean-Persian Empire, while the goat represented the Greek King Antiochus Epiphanes, who persecuted the Jews and profaned the temple during the Maccabean period (168 B.C.).

In chapter 9, Daniel had a vision as he prayed and read Jeremiah's prophecy of 70 years of exile. The angel Gabriel revealed that there would be an additional 70 weeks of years before the coming of the Messiah, his death, and the end of the sacrificial system:

"Seventy weeks are decreed about your people and your holy city, to finish the transgression, to put an end to sin, and to atone for iniquity, to bring in everlasting righteousness, to seal both vision and prophet, and to anoint a most holy place.

Know therefore and understand that from the going out of the word to restore and build Jerusalem to the coming of an anointed one, a prince, there shall be seven weeks. Then for sixty-two weeks it shall be built again with squares and moat, but in a troubled time. And after the sixty-two weeks, an anointed one

shall be cut off and shall have nothing.
And the people of the prince who is to come
shall destroy the city and the sanctuary.
Its end shall come with a flood, and to the end there shall be war.
Desolations are decreed.

And he shall make a strong covenant with many for one week,
and for half of the week he shall put an end to sacrifice and offering.
And on the wing of abominations shall come one who makes desolate,
until the decreed end is poured out on the desolator."
(Daniel 9:24-27)

In the final vision, Daniel learned that the battles he saw on Earth mirrored a war in the heavens, fought by the angels of God. Daniel saw the final battle, which would end in triumph for the Lord and his people. The faithful dead were to be raised to new life and given the glory of God:

"At that time shall arise Michael,
the great prince who has charge of your people.
And there shall be a time of trouble,
such as never has been since there was a nation till that time.
But at that time your people shall be delivered,
everyone whose name shall be found written in the book.
And many of those who sleep in the dust of the earth shall awake,
some to everlasting life, and some to shame and everlasting contempt.
And those who are wise shall shine like the brightness of the sky above;
and those who turn many to righteousness, like the stars forever
and ever."
(Daniel 12:1-3)

EZRA: Cyrus' Edict

After the overthrow of the Babylonian empire, the Persians allow the people to return to their homeland. The Book of Ezra begins at the end of the 70-year Babylonian exile. It represents a crucial moment in Israel's history, as the captivity, exile, return and restoration of the Jewish nation fulfilled prophecies found earlier in Scripture.

Ezra is part of a narrative series, following 1 and 2 Chronicles and preceding the book of Nehemiah (however, most scholars believe

Book of Ezra:

Two main issues faced by the returning exiles

Outline of Ezra:

First Return from Exile and the Rebuilding of the Temple (1:1-6:22)

Ezra's Return to Jerusalem (7:1-8:30)

Ezra's Reforms (9:1-10:44)

that they do not all share the same author). The events of Ezra date back to approximately 537 B.C., the first year of Cyrus' reign, while the book was written nearly a century later, between 460-440 B.C.

First Return from Exile and the Rebuilding of the Temple

The opening verses of Ezra are strikingly similar to the closing verses of 2 Chronicles. In both passages, Cyrus, a pagan king who was nonetheless moved by the Lord, issued an edict permitting the Israelites to return to Jerusalem and rebuild their temple:

"In the first year of Cyrus king of Persia,
that the word of the LORD by the mouth of Jeremiah might be fulfilled,
the LORD stirred up the spirit of Cyrus king of Persia,
so that he made a proclamation throughout all his kingdom and also put it in writing:
'Thus says Cyrus king of Persia: The LORD, the God of heaven, has given me all the kingdoms of the earth,
and he has charged me to build him a house at Jerusalem, which is in Judah.
Whoever is among you of all his people, may his God be with him, and let him go up to Jerusalem, which is in Judah,
and rebuild the house of the LORD, the God of Israel
—he is the God who is in Jerusalem.'"
(Ezra 1:1-3)

Fig. 6. *Cyrus Cylinder*. Akkadian cuneiform script. Discovered in Babylon in the 6th century by Hormuzd Rassam. British Museum, London.

Years of exile had taken their toll on the worship of their Lord. Though many of the Israelites, such as Daniel and Esther, continued to trust in the Lord and did their best to serve him faithfully in these trying times, worshipping and offering sacrifices to Yahweh in the Temple as prescribed in the Torah was not possible. The Jews who did worship regularly could not, for much of their exile, do so openly, without fear of persecution.

This experience had humbled God's chosen people. Much as Joshua's generation, who had known nothing but the wilderness, followed the rebellious generation of Moses, the generations that knew only exile trusted more fully in God than the one that was handed over to the Babylonians. God saw this, and he knew that his people were

152 Old Covenant and Ancient Israel

ready. Through Cyrus, he brought them home.

The first order of business was to rebuild the altar, so that they could offer their burnt offerings (Ezra 3:2). When this was completed, the people held the Festival of the Tabernacle. During this incredible nine-day feast, they took palm branches and waved them in the air as a symbol of worship to God. When Jesus, five hundred years later, entered Jerusalem on a donkey, his disciples also waved palm branches. Like the Israelites' return from exile, the triumphal entry of the king of the Jews was a fulfillment of Scripture and a sign of God's goodness and blessing, which Christians continue to celebrate every year on Palm Sunday.

When the festival came to an end, the Israelites at last began the long-awaited reconstruction of their temple.

"And all the people shouted with a great shout when they praised the LORD,
because the foundation of the house of the LORD was laid.
But many of the priests and Levites and heads of fathers' houses, old men who had seen the first house,
wept with a loud voice when they saw the foundation of this house being laid, though many shouted aloud for joy,
so that the people could not distinguish the sound of the joyful shout from the sound of the people's weeping,
for the people shouted with a great shout,
and the sound was heard far away."
(Ezra 3:11-13)

But not everyone was as enthusiastic about the return of the Jewish temple. The enemies of the Israelites believed that Jerusalem was a wicked city with a long history of insubordination that would rebel against the Persian king whenever an opportunity arose. They attempted to sabotage the reconstruction throughout the reigns of Cyrus, Artaxerxes and Darius:

"Then the people of the land discouraged the people of Judah and made them afraid to build and bribed counselors against them to frustrate their purpose, all the days of Cyrus king of Persia, even until the reign of Darius king of Persia."
(Ezra 4:4-5)

Though the Israelites experienced a number of setbacks, the prophets Haggai and Zechariah inspired them to finish their work, for the

Lord was on their side. With God's help, the people finished their work in time to celebrate Passover in 515 B.C.

Ezra's Return to Jerusalem

Ezra was an itinerant priest and teacher of the law. Like a modern-day traveling evangelist who comes to town for a big tent revival, Ezra would go from town to town, on a mission from the Lord to bring the people back to obedience to the scriptures.

With the support of King Artaxerxes, Ezra brought hundreds of people with him back to Jerusalem, and, seeing much sin, began a series of reforms.

Ezra's Reforms

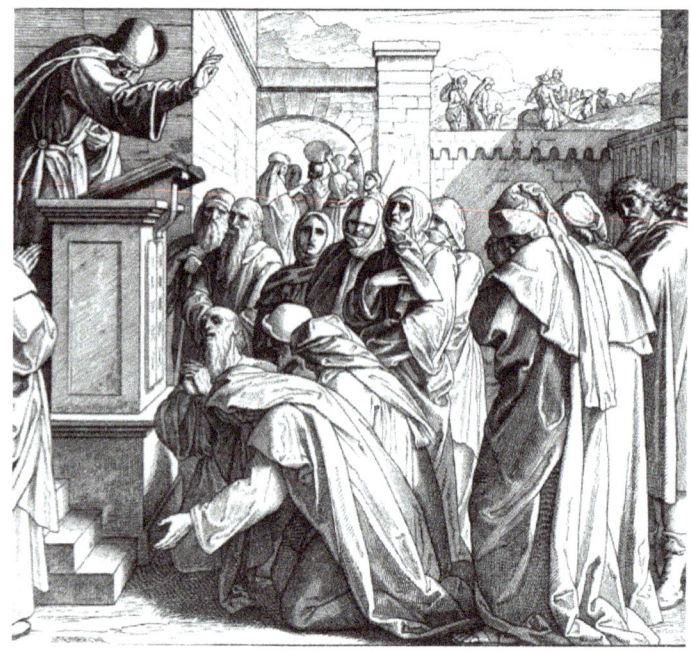

Fig. 7. Schnorr von Carolsfeld, Julius. *Ezra Proclaims the Law.* 1853. Engraving. Pitts Theological Library, Emory University, Atlanta.

"After these things had been done, the officials approached me and said, 'The people of Israel and the priests and the Levites have not separated themselves from the peoples of the lands with their abominations, from the Canaanites, the Hittites, the Perizzites, the Jebusites, the Ammonites, the Moabites, the Egyptians, and the Amorites. For they have taken some of their daughters to be wives for themselves and for their sons, so that the holy race has mixed itself with the peoples of the lands. And in this faithlessness the hand of the officials and chief men has been foremost.'"
(Ezra 9:1-2)

Ezra encountered an offense against the Lord that needed to end: the mixing of God's people with pagan nations. These people were making sacrifices to idols, and their men were marrying their own daughters and sisters.

This brought Ezra to his knees in repentance. He spoke the truth to the people and called for forgiveness and change. The people responded to Ezra's brokenness with revival, because God had softened and changed their hearts.

NEHEMIAH: Rebuilding and Renewal

The exile was partially over. The temple had been rebuilt and the people had begun to return to the Lord. But the work of rebuilding was not done, for the walls of Jerusalem were still in ruins and the people were not fully organized for worship of the Lord. So God put it on the heart of his servant Nehemiah to lead the people of Judea in rebuilding the walls of Jerusalem. This rebuilding represented a greater rebuilding of confidence in Yahweh's provision and mercy, and a renewal of the covenant he had made with his people long ago.

The book of Nehemiah shows two phases in Nehemiah's leadership. The first phase was leading the people in rebuilding and securing the walls of Jerusalem. In addition to fortifying the temple complex for worship, Nehemiah knew that it was important to fortify Jerusalem in order to strengthen the hearts and character of the people of Israel. Unsurprisingly, the same enemies who had feared a strong Israel would try to sabotage the rebuilding of the city, though they would not prevail.

The second phase was restoring the people's spiritual fortifications through the renewal of their covenant with Yahweh. It began with reading the Torah and making great offerings of thanksgiving and repentance. This phase was also vulnerable to worldly influences and human sin.

Fig. 8. Repin, Ilya. *Cry of the Prophet Jeremiah on the Ruins of Jerusalem.* 1870. Oil on paperboard. Tretyakov Gallery, Moscow.

It was only through Nehemiah's godly leadership that both the physical and spiritual restoration projects were kept on track. To this day, Nehemiah's example is a useful resource for any Christian leader who wants to take a part in reforming, renewing and rebuilding the kingdom of God in the world.

"The remnant there in the province who had survived the exile
is in great trouble and shame.
The wall of Jerusalem is broken down,
and its gates are destroyed by fire."
(Nehemiah 1:3)

Outline of Nehemiah:

Building the Walls of Jerusalem (1-7)

Renewing the Covenant (8-13)]

The Heart of the Problem

The first two chapters reveal the heart of Nehemiah. Nehemiah's official profession was cupbearer to the king of the Persian empire in the city of Susa. But God had set his heart on the people of Judah and with Jerusalem.

Nehemiah heard news that the Israelites that had already returned to their homes were in *"great trouble and shame,"* and that Jerusalem's wall and gates were utterly destroyed. (Nehemiah 1:3) When he heard this, Nehemiah felt great sadness. His response was to weep, mourn, and fast for days, and pray to the Lord for forgiveness and restoration:

"Let your ear be attentive and your eyes open,
to hear the prayer of your servant that I now pray before you day
and night for the people of Israel your servants,
confessing the sins of the people of Israel,
which we have sinned against you."
(Nehemiah 1:6)

Nehemiah began his reform effort in repentance and prayer. Yahweh, seeing his servant's honesty and humility, removed great obstacles through his providence. The first potential obstacle was the Persian king, Nehemiah's employer. Amazingly, however, the king not only let Nehemiah return to Jerusalem, he even wrote letters offering his protection and financial support! Truly, Nehemiah's cup ran over. When Nehemiah arrived in Jerusalem to survey the task before him, he met Sanballat the Horonite and Tobiah the Ammonite. These two men were greatly displeased that *"someone had come to seek the welfare of the people of Israel"* (Nehemiah 2:10) and spearheaded opposition to the reconstruction of Jerusalem.

But Nehemiah did not fear these men. He made a public announcement, in which he gave his vision for a rebuilt Jerusalem:

"Then I said to them, 'You see the trouble we are in,
how Jerusalem lies in ruins with its gates burned.
Come, let us build the wall of Jerusalem,
that we may no longer suffer derision.'"
(Nehemiah 2:17)

Rebuilding and Resistance

The vision of Nehemiah proved compelling. The people set their hearts and hands to the task of repairing the walls of Jerusalem, and men (and women!) came from far and wide to rebuild and raise the gates and walls, district by district, section by section, brick by brick.

But their work was not without opposition:

*"Now when Sanballat heard that we were building the wall,
he was angry and greatly enraged, and he jeered at the Jews.
And he said in the presence of his brothers and of the army of Samaria,
'What are these feeble Jews doing? Will they restore it for themselves?
Will they sacrifice? Will they finish up in a day?
Will they revive the stones out of the heaps of rubbish, and burned ones at that?'"*
(Nehemiah 4:1-2)

Nehemiah was determined not to give up, however, and he encouraged the people to stand tall. He instructed the people to resist the opposition in several important ways.

First, they gave over their enemies to the Lord and prayed for his protection. Second, they armed themselves and showed themselves ready to defend their work, their families and their homes. Third, they continued to rebuild, showing themselves to be strong to the task of rebuilding.

Fig. 9. *Working on the walls of Jerusalem even under threat.* "Treasures of the Bible." 1894. Henry Davenport Northrop.

A major issue, though, was that the opposition did not only come from outside the community, but also from within. As Nehemiah learned of the broken walls, he also learned of the broken relationships in the family of God. Nehemiah called on the people to keep covenant with one another and repent of their sin and ordered them to end the practices that had contributed to the breakdown of community: the usurious taxation and enslavement of one another.

*"Yet you have been righteous in all that has come upon us,
for you have dealt faithfully and we have acted wickedly."*
(Nehemiah 9:33)

Nehemiah also faced a plot hatched against him: Sanballat and Tobiah made a last-ditch effort to thwart the rebuilding by seeking to ambush Nehemiah by using intimidation and deception. Through false prophecy, they attempted to trick him into entering the Holy of Holies, so that he would be struck down by God. Yet Nehemiah was protected because he feared God more than men:

"But I said, 'Should such a man as I run away?
And what man such as I could go into the temple and live?
I will not go in.'"
(Nehemiah 6:11)

Despite all of the opposition they faced in rebuilding the walls, gates and doors of Jerusalem, Nehemiah and the people prevailed in the end. Chapter 7 takes inventory of the people and resources of the rebuilt Jerusalem. With the boundaries of Jerusalem restored, Nehemiah's attention now turned to the restoration of the covenant within the hearts and minds of the people.

Covenant Restoration

The rebuilt walls of Jerusalem provided a safe and sacred space in which the remnant of Judah could be rebuilt as the covenant people of God. Unfortunately, the covenant relationship with Yahweh was in great disrepair.

In Chapter 8, we read of the scribe Ezra, who assembled the people within the walls to hear once again the words of the Torah, which had been largely forgotten. The people responded with faith and a teachable spirit, and even restored the festival of the booths, which had not been celebrated in Israel since the time of Joshua!

The restoration is akin to a new exodus and conquest. The remnant had wandered through the wilderness of the Babylonian exile because of their sin; and yet, God showed mercy to them—just as he had done in the days of Moses.

Following the confession of their sins, the people recommitted themselves to covenant faithfulness and offerings to the Lord.

"We will not neglect the house of our God."
(Nehemiah 10:39)

Restoring the House of Our God

The testimony of the people was to keep the covenant and maintain the temple through faithful worship, offerings and tithes. Chapters 10 and 11 provide another inventory of all those who renewed the covenant and offered to live within and just outside the walls of Jerusalem in faithful service of the Lord: gatekeepers, priests, singers and temple servants.

Faithlessness:

Allowed the foreigner to dwell in a temple room

Failed to bring appropriate tithes and offerings to the Levites

Bought and sold on the Sabbath

Intermarried with Ammonites and Moabites

However, just as there was opposition to the rebuilding of the physical walls, so too was there opposition and sabotage to the spiritual walls of Jerusalem. Some of the people made compromises in their commitments, which required Nehemiah to step up and quickly put a stop to it.

For example, Eliashab, the priest in charge of the chambers of the temple complex, was related to the Ammonite Tobiah, who had caused so much trouble for Nehemiah. Eliashab initially allowed Tobiah to dwell in a temple room, but Nehemiah kicked him out and restored the chamber for its godly purpose.

The Israelites also failed to bring the appropriate offerings to the Levites, forcing them to abandon worship in order to provide for their families. In addition, they were lax in their keeping of the Sabbath, and would conduct business on that holy day. There was also the lingering problem of intermarriage with Gentiles. But in all of these cases, Nehemiah led the people to repentance and held them accountable to covenant faithfulness.

"Thus I cleansed them from everything foreign,
and I established the duties of the priests and Levites, each in his work;
and I provided for the wood offering at appointed times,
and for the firstfruits.
Remember me, O my God, for good."
(Nehemiah 13:30-31)

CHAPTER 8 NOTES:

CHAPTER 9
The Wisdom of Israel: The Fear of the Lord

Objective: The maturing disciple of Jesus will understand that the fear of the Lord is the beginning of wisdom.

The final aspect of living into God's covenants is wisdom. How do we make decisions rooted in truth and insight? How do we serve God faithfully, without falling prey to our own foolishness?

The Old Testament, in addition to the many examples of men and women acting in wisdom that we have seen in the preceding chapters, contains several books dedicated, in some form or another, specifically to wisdom: Job, Ecclesiastes, Psalms, and Proverbs.

Have you considered my servant Job?

There is a very simple question that human beings have struggled with for thousands of years. It has led many to doubt God's goodness, and even his existence. It is one of the leading justifications given by those who do not have faith in God. That question is articulated by a Greek philosopher named Epicurus. He states:

"Either God wants to abolish evil, and cannot;
or he can, but does not want to;
or he cannot and does not want to.
If he wants to, but cannot, he is impotent.
If he can, and does not want to, he is wicked.
But, if God both can and wants to abolish evil,
then how come evil is in the world?"
(Epicurus, philosopher (340-270 B.C.)

Fig. 1. de Ribera, Jusepe. *Job on the Ash Heap.* c. Jativa, Valencia c. 1591 - 1652 Naples. Oil on canvas.

theodicy—(noun)
the·od·i·cy \ thē-ˈä-də-sē
defense of God's goodness and omnipotence in view of the existence of evil
Merriam-Webster Dictionary

It would seem logical that a good God would prevent unjust human suffering, and all evil along with it. Since he does not, he must be either cruel, weak, or nonexistent.

It is indeed a difficult question—and there is a temptation among people of faith to rush to defend God with answers that have not been fully thought out. But the question remains and is known in theology as the problem of evil.

God, however, has not remained silent about the problem of evil. In fact, there is an entire book of the Bible that wrestles directly with it: the book of Job. It is a unique and valuable book, unlike any other in Scripture, and its message will resonate with anyone who has struggled with unjust suffering.

THE BOOK OF JOB

Though the author of Job is unknown, we know that he is a Hebrew because he calls God Yahweh. The story, however, does not take place in Israel, but in a land called Uz, which would have been in Edom or southern Arabia. It is set around the same time as Abraham. It is unknown to us whether Job, the book's protagonist and namesake, was an actual person or rather a character in an (extended) parable, of the kind that Jesus would one day tell his disciples.

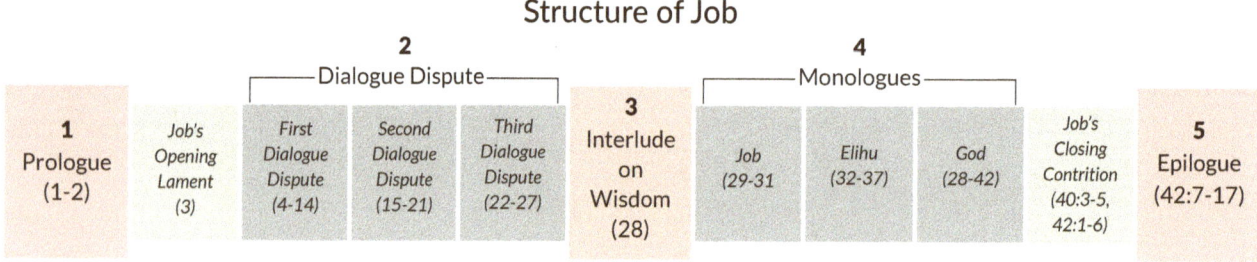

Job's Lament and Crisis

The book tells us that Job was a good man, a pious and faithful servant of God. Yahweh had blessed him with a wife, ten children, many servants, and over ten thousand animals (Job 1:1-3). But Satan questioned Job's loyalty to God, telling Yahweh that Job only worshipped him because of the blessings he had received, and that he would curse God if those blessings were to be taken away. (Job 1:9-11)

So God told Satan,

"Behold, all that he has is in your hand.
Only against him do not stretch out your hand."
(Job 1:12)

With that, Job began to experience deep personal suffering. His children, his servants, and his animals were killed in several bewildering events: a house collapsing, a "fire of God," a Sabean raid. He had lost almost all of the blessings in his life.

When Job remained faithful to God even in his great pain, Satan told God that Job was only faithful because he himself was spared from death or sickness. If God were to inflict physical pain on Job himself, then he would curse God. So Satan gave Job "loathsome boils" all over his body. Job's wife and counselors, angry at the injustice of his lot, would encourage him to break his relationship with God over loss, pain and suffering.

A Book of Conflict

Four conflicts arise in the first few chapters of Job. The first is the secret conflict between God and Satan. There is an assumption within the problem of evil: that a good God should and will consistently bless the righteous and deserving and punish the wicked and undeserving. This understanding of who God is (or should be) is popular even among many Christians, especially those in so-called "Prosperity Gospel" circles. After all, in what sense could God be good if the world he created were not just?

Fig. 3. Giaquinto, Corrado. *Satan Before the Lord.* c. 1750. Oil on canvas. Vatican Museums.

The conversation between God and Satan shows that such a view is problematic. Satan turned the assumption on its head: what if the truth is that people are righteous and godly only because they receive blessings (which in turn encourage more good behavior)? In other words, faithfulness to God is a purely transactional relationship—like any job, if we do what he asks, he will pay us for it. Nothing more than that, for there is nothing resembling love there.

Job had no idea that this debate is occurring. This is the root of the second conflict, the one that he had with God. Through his servant, God sought to show that true faithfulness is not a relationship of transactions, but a relationship of love. There is a deeper question in the conflict: do people—can people—really love and obey God even in the absence of material blessings and the presence of material curses? From a heavenly perspective, what was at stake is the integrity of the righteous in the face of hardship. But from Job's perspective, what was at stake is knowing whether God is just, or even cares about his suffering at all. A God who did not care about human beings would indeed be a God who *should* be cursed, for there would no goodness in such a God!

> **Job's Faithfulness is Tested:**
>
> *Satan's accusations*
>
> *Job's integrity in loss of family and property*
>
> *Satan's further accusations*
>
> *Job's integrity in personal suffering*
>
> *The coming of the counselors*

The third conflict is between Job and his counselors. These supposed friends pushed their own flawed understandings of suffering and theology to extremes—a warning that there is no foolproof or complete explanation of the problem of evil available to humans. The book of Proverbs tells the reader to "Trust in the Lord with all your heart, and do not lean on your own understanding." (Proverbs 3:5) But Job's counselors lacked the humility and the wisdom to do so. In their logic, they falsely accused Job of wrongdoing—what other explanation could there be for his punishment? In the end, they accomplished far more harm than good.

The fourth conflict is an internal one: Job wrestled with his thoughts that pulled him in different directions. He trusted and feared God, and yet he did not understand why this was all happening. He believed that he was innocent, and he believed that God was sovereign and just. Job despaired, even to the point of cursing the day of his birth.

Job and His Counselors

At first, Job's counselors actually did well. They recognized Job's pain and simply sat with him, saying nothing:

"Now when Job's three friends heard
of all this evil that had come upon him,
they came each from his own place,
Eliphaz the Temanite, Bildad the Shuhite,
and Zophar the Naamathite.
They made an appointment together
to come to show him sympathy and comfort him.
... And they sat with him on the ground
seven days and seven nights,
and no one spoke a word to him,
for they saw that his suffering was very great."
(Job 2:11, 13)

But their sympathy broke down when they heard Job's words. Job cursed himself, and he cursed the day and night of his birth. This curse was rooted in his deep misery. To Job, death would be far better than the living hell he was experiencing.

"How then will you comfort me with empty nothings?
There is nothing left of your answers but falsehood."
(Job 21:34)

Job and his counselors were wrestling both with the problem of evil and with two known truths:
- There is one living and true God of infinite power, wisdom and goodness;
- Man is not infinite in power, wisdom or goodness.

Job, in his prayers, asked the unanswered questions. He sought vindication, and he sought an advocate—a redeemer—who could make a case to the Lord on his behalf. Job was far more concerned about his own relationship with God than his counselors' critique of his integrity, which he knew was not in doubt.

Where is Wisdom?

The profound questions raised in the Book of Job can only be answered with great wisdom. But where is wisdom to be found? The hinge passage of the book is an interlude poem on wisdom. It explains that wisdom is not found anywhere on earth or in the heavens—it is only found in the fear of the Lord!

Fig. 4. Carrasco, Gonzalo. *Job on the Dunghill.* 1881. Oil on canvas. Museo Nacional de Arte, Mexico City.

"And he said to man, 'Behold, the fear of the Lord, that is wisdom, and to turn away from evil is understanding.'"
(Job 28:28)

That statement may seem strange to us: isn't wisdom an inner power, understanding something that other people do not, being able to make good decisions and judgments *without* having to rely on the input of others? King Solomon, after all, was considered wise because he made Israel prosperous and prestigious, and he did so through his own wisdom, not through anyone else's. But the poem says that wisdom means relying on God's understanding rather than one's own, "wise" as our understanding may seem. Solomon had forgotten that God had given him that wisdom and leaned more and more on his own understanding. And as we saw, the prosperity and prestige of his kingdom died with him. God's wisdom on the other hand, is everlasting. That is why true wisdom is the fear of the Lord, paradoxical as that may sound.

Principles of Lament:

Patience and Faith to Despondency and Depression

Irrational: the Uncreation

Asks Unanswered Questions

Seeks Vindication

Seeks an Advocate

"Then Job answered the Lord and said:
'Behold, I am of small account; what shall I answer you?
I lay my hand on my mouth.
I have spoken once, and I will not answer;
twice, but I will proceed no further.'"
(Job 40:3-5)

Fig. 5. Blake, William. *Job, his Wife and his Friends.* c. 1785. Ink and watercolor on paper. Tate Britain, London.

Principles of Bad Counsel:

Lecturing rather than listening

Failing to empathize

Answering the questions

Applying theology without understanding

Defending God, not Job

Having a low view of the value of humanity

"Reason's last step is the recognition that there are an infinite number of things which are beyond it."
Blaise Pascal, *Pensées*

The Three Monologues

Job's three monologue speeches at the end of the book (Job 26-31) move the questions toward a kind of resolution. Job, wanting a direct answer from God, made his final case before God. He believed he has received unjust treatment. Like a lawyer, he laid out his case before God, demonstrating point by point that he had kept himself from evil and been a person of righteousness.

Elihu Makes a Speech

A new counselor, Elihu, is introduced. He provided the best insight that human counsel had to offer. Elihu rebuked the counselors and Job: he believed that the counselors in their wickedness accused Job wrongly, but he also argued that Job had crossed a line in his words to God. He reminded Job that God was by his very nature fully sovereign and just, no matter what Job thought. This monologue sets up God's answer to Job (Job 38).

God Answers Job

When it came, God's answer was truly terrifying; out of a whirlwind theophany (or divine apparition), he challenged Job to a wrestling match!

God proclaimed his wisdom and power in all creation. The purpose of God's speech was to reveal that there is so much about the creation that humanity cannot possibly understand. The origins of the universe remain a mystery to humanity, and though we observe and speculate and theorize, we only know the tiniest fraction of how it all came into being.

Job, to his credit, responds humbly. God then proclaims his absolute justice. While there are evil creatures in creation, like the behemoth and the leviathan, ultimately these creatures are under God's control. Job will simply have to trust God and his goodness. Job repents his arrogance and humbles his heart before God, and his wealth and blessings are restored to him (though the pain of his previous losses, we can imagine, do not simply go away; he must live with them).

ECCLESIASTES

"What does man gain by all the toil at which he toils under the sun?"

(Ecclesiastes 1:3)

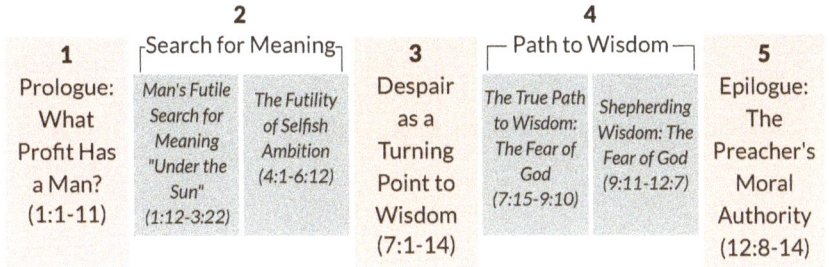

Structure of Ecclesiastes

This question can be a difficult one for many people. We work hard, We try to survive. We create lives for ourselves. But why? What is the point? It can make us question everything we do and everything we are if we do not have a good answer. A biblical book which provides surprising wisdom on this point is the book of Ecclesiastes. The book's title comes from the Greek word *ekklesia,* or "assembly." It is a rough translation of the original Hebrew for the preacher, the one who calls the assembly, the *qohelet*.

While the book's author, traditionally called the Preacher, is not explicitly named, several verses within the text point to King Solomon. This is the understanding of most Christians and Jews, though not all modern interpreters agree. The author chose to go unnamed, and with good reason: the important figure is not himself, but the true author of the collected wisdom, the *"one Shepherd"* (Job 12:11).

Ecclesiastes centers on the Hebrew word hebel, which can alternately be translated as "vanity" or "vapor." The Preacher reflects upon the meaning and purpose of life. He concludes that, apart from God, the human search for meaning in life is no more fruitful than grasping at a vapor, and the vanity of vanities.

The book of Ecclesiastes can be separated into three parts. The Preacher first ponders the futility of pursuing wisdom apart from God. Then, the poem in the middle of the book (Ecclesiastes 3:1-8) is a hinge, discussing godly despair in human uncertainty and folly. Finally, the Preacher reflects on the "work of God" and concludes that wisdom ultimately is found not in man, but in the fear of God.

*"And I applied my heart to seek and to search out by wisdom
all that is done under heaven.
It is an unhappy business that God has given
to the children of man to be busy with.
I have seen everything that is done under the sun,
and behold, all is vanity and a striving after wind."*
(Ecclesiastes 1:13-14)

> "There is but one living and true God ... of infinite power, wisdom, and goodness ..."
> Article 1, Book of Common Prayer

Prologue: What Profit Has a Man?

*"Vanity of vanities, says the Preacher, vanity of vanities!
All is vanity."*
(Ecclesiastes 1:2)

The prologue names several vanity cycles, including life and death; reproduction; the daily cycles of the sun, wind, and water. Is there any purpose to all of it? Or is it all *hebel*, vanity? The Preacher sets out to answer this question.

Man's Futile Search for Meaning "Under the Sun"

The Preacher observes that there is a marked futility in the human condition. The more he considers the purpose for human labor and existence, the more vexing the question becomes. His own life is a perfect example: he would spend his days pursuing pleasures and the so-called finer things of life. *"And whatever my eyes desired I did not keep from them."* (Ecclesiastes 2:10)

Over time, however, he came to realize that this was a vain exercise from which he gained nothing. And he decided to find answers in human wisdom and knowledge and insight. But again he found nothing of value in his selfish quest for wisdom or labor.

God has ordered everything and given *"a time for every matter under heaven."* (Ecclesiastes 3:1) The ultimate purposes are recognizable, and yet are elusive:

*"He has made everything beautiful in its time.
Also, he has put eternity into man's heart,
yet so that he cannot find out what God has done
from the beginning to the end."*
(Ecclesiastes 3:11)

God's purposes for man's labor and his destiny for man seem completely inscrutable.

"For when dreams increase and words grow many, there is vanity;
but God is the one you must fear."
(Ecclesiastes 5:7)

The Futility of Selfish Ambition

The Preacher turns to a reflection on the futility of human pursuit of selfish ambition. This pursuit leads to bitter tyranny and oppression, for man's envy is self-consuming: *"The fool folds his hands and eats his own flesh."* (Ecclesiastes 4:5) Selfish ambition, rather than giving a person everything they need and want, leads only to a lonely alienation and foolish self-centered existence:

"Again, I saw vanity under the sun:
one person who has no other, either son or brother,
yet there is no end to all his toil,
and his eyes are never satisfied with riches
so that he never asks,
'For whom am I toiling and depriving myself of pleasure?'
This also is vanity and an unhappy business."
(Ecclesiastes 4:7-8)

The sin of selfish ambition is a sin of presumption upon the grace of God: we tell ourselves that we deserve what we want, and God should give it to us. This leads to arrogance in our decisions, and a lack of recognition that the dreams and plans we make for ourselves are often not the ways and plans God has in mind.

"Surely there is not a righteous man on earth
who does good and never sins."
(Ecclesiastes 7:20)

Ultimately, the selfish pursuit of more and more wealth will prove to be unsatisfying and stressful. There is no point at which one is perfectly satisfied with his wealth, for one could always have more and do more. And the more one owns, the more worries he will have, because there is more to lose. And in the end, it will all inevitably be lost. *"As he came from his mother's womb he shall go again, naked as he came, and shall take nothing for his toil that he may carry away in his hand."* (Ecclesiastes 5:15) The moral? Hold wealth loosely, enjoy it while you have it—and count your blessings as a gift from God!

"For who knows what is good for man
while he lives the few days of his vain life,
which he passes like a shadow?
For who can tell man what will be
after him under the sun?"
(Ecclesiastes 6:12)

Despair as a Turning Point to Wisdom

The Preacher places a poetic hinge at the center of the book. The poem calls the reader to despair—a note which may at first sound discordant with messages of hope elsewhere in Scripture. The first half of the book has lead the reader to ask: what indeed is the point of it all if life here is so uncertain and all of our work ultimately leads to no earthly gain?

Only when we become so thoroughly disillusioned with ourselves and our selfish ambition do we think to turn outward toward God. The answer is not found in self and the works of our hands, but in the work of God and his wisdom.

"For the protection of wisdom is like the protection of money,
and the advantage of knowledge is that wisdom preserves the
life of him who has it. Consider the work of God: who can make
straight what he has made crooked?"
(Ecclesiastes 7:12-13)

The True Path to Wisdom: The Fear of God

As the book of Job also told us, the key to wisdom is found in trust and fear in the sovereign God. We may not understand his ways or purposes in our prosperities and adversities, but we must trust him anyway.

We should be humble in our own self-estimation. We are hopelessly inadequate in our own depravity, and we are our own worst barriers to discerning wisdom. *"God made man upright, but they have sought out many schemes."* (Ecclesiastes 7:29) So fear of God is man's only hope.

"Though a sinner does evil a hundred times and prolongs his life,
yet I know that it will be well with those who fear God,
because they fear before him.
But it will not be well with the wicked,
neither will he prolong his days like a shadow,
because he does not fear before God."
(Ecclesiastes 8:12-13)

Shepherding Wisdom: The Work of God

The Preacher cautions his reader to live the wisdom of the fear of the Lord holding loosely to life in a fallen world. There is much that will happen in this life that will seem unfair or nonsensical. But the wisdom you shepherd into your heart and life will prove to be a blessing to you. Wisdom's advantage is dismissed by fools, and will be forfeited by those who give their life to folly. Life is filled with adversity, but our call is to steward the wisdom of God, found in the work of God.

Epilogue: The Preacher's Moral Authority

"Besides being wise, the Preacher also taught the people knowledge,
weighing and studying and arranging many proverbs with great care.
The Preacher sought to find words of delight,
and uprightly he wrote words of truth.
The words of the wise are like goads,
and like nails firmly fixed are the collected sayings;
they are given by one Shepherd.
My son, beware of anything beyond these.
Of making many books there is no end,
and much study is a weariness of the flesh.
The end of the matter; all has been heard.
Fear God and keep his commandments,
for this is the whole duty of man.
For God will bring every deed into judgment,
with every secret thing, whether good or evil."
(Ecclesiastes 12:9-14)

Psalms

The book of Psalms is one of the most easily recognized in the Bible. Its psalms are quoted liberally in the Gospels and the rest of the New Testament, and they have inspired countless hymns and songs of worship over thousands of years. And with the exceptions of the Lord's Prayer and the beginning of Genesis, there is perhaps no biblical passage more familiar to Christians around the world than Psalm 23 *("The Lord is my shepherd, I shall not want…")*.

King David is credited with writing 73 of the 150 psalms, while the others are either attributed to minor figures or anonymous. There are all kinds of psalms: psalms of praise, of pleading, of anger, of repentance. Like the relationship between God and his people, however, there is an arc which bends toward hope and salvation in the ordering of the book of Psalms. They both ultimately point to the death and resurrection of Jesus Christ. After all, Jesus, in his moment of pain and despair, quoted Psalm 22 on the cross:

"My God, my God, why have you forsaken me?"
(Psalm 22:1, Matthew 27:46, Mark 15:34)

But in speaking of his triumph over evil and death, and the coming of the Kingdom of God, Jesus calls on a later psalm, Psalm 118:

"The stone that the builders rejected
has become the cornerstone.
This was the Lord's doing;
and it is marvelous in our eyes."
(Psalm 118:22-33, Matthew 21:42, Mark 12:10-11, Luke 20:17)

CHAPTER 9 NOTES:

CHAPTER 9 NOTES:

www.ingramcontent.com/pod-product-compliance
Lightning Source LLC
Chambersburg PA
CBHW042014120526
44592CB00043B/2857